EXPERIENCE
THE AMALFI COAST
LIKE A FIRST
TIMER

A Guide To Sorrento, Positano, Capri, Naples, Pompeii & other Regions

John H. Leon

Copyright © by John H. Leon 2025.

All rights reserved.

Except for brief quotations used in critical reviews and other non-commercial uses permitted by copyright law, no part of this publication may be copied, distributed, or transmitted in any way without the publisher's prior written consent, including by photocopying, recording, or other electronic or mechanical methods.

The use of any trademarks or brands mentioned in this book is solely for the purpose of clarification and is not intended to imply any affiliation with the respective owners of those marks or brands.

Map of Amalfi

Click here to View the Map of Amalfi (For e-book readers)

Scan the QR Code below with your mobile phone's Camera to View the Map of Amalfi (For Paperback Readers).

TABLE OF CONTENTS

Map of Amalfi
INTRODUCTION
    Geographic Highlights of the Amalfi Coast and Its Diverse Regions
    History and Culture of the Amalfi Coast: A Tapestry of Mediterranean Traditions
CHAPTER 1 Essential Tips for Travelers
    Visa Guidelines and Entry Requirements for Italy
    Health and Safety Updates Across the Amalfi Coast
    What to Pack: Amalfi Coast Edition
    Budgeting for Your Trip: Expenses on the Amalfi Coast
    Optimal Travel Times to Visit Different Towns
    Understanding Local Culture and Social Norms
    Connectivity: Wi-Fi Availability, SIM Cards, and Communication
    Essential Travel Apps and Websites for Italy
    Basic Italian Phrases for Travelers
CHAPTER 2 Arrival and Transportation

Arriving on the Amalfi Coast: Major Airports and Entry Points

Getting Around: Public Transportation, Including Buses, Ferries, and Scooters

Navigating the Amalfi Coast: Car Rentals, Taxis, and Ride-Sharing Services

Tips for Walking and Cycling Along the Coastal Roads

CHAPTER 3 Where to Stay

Accommodation Ranges: From Luxury Resorts to Budget Hostels

Characteristic Boutique Hotels and Historic Stays in Major Towns

Family-Friendly Hotels and Vacation Resorts

Distinctive Stays: Cliffside Villas and Seaside Bungalows

Reservation Insights and Preferred Booking Platforms

CHAPTER 4 Food and Dining

Traditional Italian Dishes to Try on the Amalfi Coast

Premier Dining Spots from Positano to Ravello

Best Restaurants for Local Seafood and Mediterranean Flavors

Cafes and Gelaterias

Vegetarian, Vegan, and Gluten-Free Options
Culinary Courses and Food Tours
CHAPTER 5 Major Towns and Attractions
Positano: Colorful Villas and Chic Beachfront
Amalfi: Historical Sites and the Famous Cathedral
Atrani: Charming Seaside Village with Picturesque Views
Ravello: Gardens, Villas, and Music Festivals
Sorrento: Vibrant Nightlife and Gateway to Capri
Nerano: Secluded Beaches and Culinary Excellence
Cetara: Authentic Fishing Village with Famous Anchovies
Maiori: Expansive Beaches and Historic Churches
Furore: The Famous Fjord and Unique Hiking Trails
Vietri sul Mare: Renowned Ceramics and Coastal Charm
Praiano: Serene Getaway and Stunning Sunsets
Salerno and Via dei Mercanti: Vibrant Port City with Iconic Shopping Streets
CHAPTER 6 Northern Amalfi Coast

Sorrento: Rich History and Access to Capri

Massa Lubrense: Natural Beauty and Quiet Villages

CHAPTER 7 Southern Amalfi Coast

Amalfi: Historical Gems and Cultural Highlights

Praiano: Serene Getaway and Path of the Gods

CHAPTER 8 Eastern Amalfi Coast

Minori and Maiori: Traditional Coastal Life and Lemon Groves

Salerno: Medieval History and Modern Vibe

CHAPTER 9 Western Amalfi Coast

Positano: Stunning Views and Upscale Shopping

Capri: La Dolce Vita, Shopping, and Natural Beauty

CHAPTER 10 Central Amalfi Coast

Ravello: Cultural Heart with Gardens and Classical Music

Scala: Hiking Trails and Rustic Charm

CHAPTER 11 Neighbourhoods and Hidden Gems

Discovering Lesser-Known Villages and Secluded Spots

Exploring Local Traditions and Artisanal Crafts

CHAPTER 12 Nightlife and Entertainment

The Best Spots for Evening Drinks and Live Music
Seasonal Outdoor Cinemas and Theatrical Performances
CHAPTER 13 Beyond the Amalfi Coast
Paestum: Ancient Greek Temples
Naples: Museums, Dining, and Historical Sites
Pompeii: Archaeological Site Details and Tours
Rome: Key Attractions
CHAPTER 14 Cultural Festivals and Events
Local Celebrations: Lemons and Festivals
Seasonal and Cultural Festivities: Experiencing Amalfi's Vibrant Traditions
Celebrations of Patron Saints: Festive Parades and Fireworks
Music and Art Festivals: A Blend of Traditional and Modern Events
CHAPTER 15 Outdoor Adventures
Beaches and Outdoor Activities
Water Sports: Diving, Sailing, Kayaking
Land Adventures: Hiking, Biking, and Scooter Tours
Paragliding and Aerial Views: Seeing the coast from above

Cultural Excursions: Visits to Historic Villas and Gardens

CHAPTER 16 Nature and Wildlife

Flora and Fauna: Exploring the diverse ecosystems

Eco-Tours: Guided tours focusing on sustainability and conservation

Exploring Marine Life: Snorkeling and Scuba Diving Tours

Botanical Gardens and Protected Natural Sites

CHAPTER 17 Spiritual and Wellness Retreats

Yoga and Meditation: Centers offering serene retreats

Spa Experiences: Top wellness treatments using local ingredients

CHAPTER 18 Activities for Different Travelers

Solo Explorers: Customized excursions and opportunities for social interaction

Couples: Idyllic beach walks and exclusive dining experiences

Families: Attractions suitable for children and family-friendly park visits

Senior Travelers: Accessible cultural excursions and relaxing activities

Group Outings: Custom group adventures with special discounts

Guided Tours vs. Self-Guided Explorations

CHAPTER 19 Itineraries

Organizing Day Trips to Nearby Attractions

Brief Visits: Structured 3-Day Plans in Top Towns

Extensive Weeklong Journeys: A Detailed 7-Day Guide

2-Week Comprehensive Tour of the Amalfi Coast

Free and Paid Tourist Attractions with Opening Hours

Departure Checklist and Customs Regulations

CHAPTER 20 Practical Information and Tips

Emergency Services: Medical Facilities and Contact Numbers

Consulates and Tourist Assistance in Italy

Special Occasion Planning: Weddings and Celebrations

Photography Hotspots: Capturing the Perfect Shot

Sustainable Tourism Practices on the Amalfi Coast

CONCLUSION

INTRODUCTION

The Amalfi Coast, a stretch of coastline famed for its rugged terrain, scenic beauty, and picturesque towns, is one of Italy's most striking destinations. Nestled on the southern side of Italy's Sorrentine Peninsula, this area offers a unique blend of natural beauty, history, and culture in a Mediterranean setting. Whether you're drawn by the allure of its sun-drenched landscapes, the charm of its old-world villages, or the taste of local cuisine, the Amalfi Coast promises a travel experience that is both enriching and unforgettable.

This region is not just a series of postcard-perfect scenes; it is a mosaic of diverse experiences and histories. The coast stretches roughly 50 kilometers from the busy port city of Salerno to the rocky cliffs of Sorrento. Each town along the way, from Positano to Ravello, tells its own unique story through ancient streets, bustling markets, and the warm, welcoming nature of its people. As you explore, you'll encounter a landscape steeped in history. The Amalfi Coast's roots go back to the Romans, and over the centuries, it has been shaped by various influences that are evident in its architecture, festivals, and daily life.

For those who cherish art and history, the coast offers centuries-old churches and villas, some of which are adorned with frescoes and ceramics that highlight the region's artistic heritage. Gastronomy here is a serious affair, characterized by fresh seafood, locally grown lemons, and handmade pasta, all of which are staples of Amalfi's culinary offerings.

Traveling to the Amalfi Coast also means experiencing the Mediterranean climate, which blesses the region with mild winters and warm, sun-filled summers—perfect for enjoying the stunning beaches and coastal paths that offer breathtaking views of the turquoise sea.

As we delve deeper into this guide, you'll find practical tips and insights on how to navigate this beautiful region. From understanding the best travel times and local customs to choosing the right places to stay and eat, this book is designed to provide all the information you need to make the most of your visit to the Amalfi Coast.

With every page, you will gain more knowledge about how to fully enjoy this stunning part of the world, making your travel both enjoyable and memorable. Ready to explore the Amalfi Coast with us? Let's embark on this wonderful journey together.

Geographic Highlights of the Amalfi Coast and Its Diverse Regions

Exploring the Amalfi Coast feels like stepping into a vibrant painting where every turn reveals a new splash of color—from the deep blues of the Mediterranean to the lush greens of terraced vineyards. Let me take you through the geographic highlights of this spectacular region, sharing some of my own experiences along the way to give you a true sense of its diverse beauty.

The journey begins in the west at Positano, a town that clings dramatically to the cliffs and offers stunning views of the sea. It's a place that seems to tumble down the hillside like a waterfall of colorful buildings, each one packed tightly against the next. Wandering the steep, narrow streets, I remember feeling enveloped by the vibrant architecture and the sweet scent of lemon mixed with salty sea air—a sensory overload in the best possible way. Traveling east, you'll find Amalfi, the heart of the coast and a name that echoes through history as a maritime power. Today, it's better known for its spectacular cathedral and the bustling piazza that fronts it. I've spent many afternoons here, sipping espresso at a café, watching as tourists and locals alike vied for shade under the cathedral's impressive façade.

Not far from Amalfi is Ravello, perched high above the sea, offering a retreat from the coastal buzz. I recall the tranquility of its lush gardens at Villa Rufolo, where the views stretch endlessly towards the horizon. The serenity here is palpable, making it a perfect spot to pause and reflect on the stunning natural beauty. Further down the coast lies the less frequented town of Atrani, a hidden gem just a stone's throw from Amalfi. This small town remains one of my favorite spots for its understated charm and the way it feels untouched by the tourist throngs. The compact town square, enclosed by high-rise buildings, offers an intimate glimpse of local life that is hard to find in the more popular towns. As we approach the eastern reaches of the coast, the landscape becomes rugged, leading to Salerno, a city that marks a stark contrast to the smaller towns we've passed. Here, the coast stretches out, offering a mix of modern city life with the ancient charm found in its old town sector. Walking along the Lungomare Trieste, the seaside promenade, I often find myself captivated by the lively atmosphere and the panoramic views of the distant cliffs.

Each of these regions on the Amalfi Coast has its own character and history, tied together by the stunning natural scenery that forms their backdrop. Whether it's the pastel-colored vistas of Positano, the historic grandeur of Amalfi, the serene heights of Ravello, the quiet charm of Atrani, or the vibrant urban life of Salerno, the Amalfi Coast offers a diverse range of experiences that cater to every traveler's whim.

History and Culture of the Amalfi Coast: A Tapestry of Mediterranean Traditions

The history and culture of the Amalfi Coast are intricately woven into a rich tapestry that dates back centuries, where each thread represents a story of conquests, trade, and artistry. The region's narrative began long before it became a renowned travel destination, with Amalfi at its heart, emerging as a maritime superpower in the 9th century. The maritime laws developed there, known as the "Tavole Amalfitane," were among the earliest forms of maritime codes and were adopted throughout the Mediterranean, underscoring the area's historical importance in seafaring and commerce.

The architectural and cultural landscapes of the Amalfi Coast bear the hallmarks of Byzantine, Arab, and Norman influences, reflecting the region's position as a crossroads of Mediterranean cultures. The Arab-Norman cloisters in Amalfi and the exotic motifs found in the villas of Ravello are vivid reminders of these ancient connections, showcasing a blend of artistic and architectural traditions that have shaped the local culture.

Religious festivals play a central role in community life, serving as vibrant and deeply rooted expressions of local faith and community spirit. Events such as the Festival of Sant'Andrea in Amalfi highlight this, with the saint's statue carried through crowded streets to the sea in a spectacle of devotion that binds the community together. These festivals are not just celebrations; they are profound demonstrations of generational faith and identity, embodying the spirit of the Amalfi Coast.

Culinary traditions also reveal much about the region's history, with local dishes featuring lemons, seafood, and handmade pasta like scialatielli that tie back to the land and sea.

Limoncello, a sweet lemon liqueur made locally, exemplifies the agricultural bounty of the coast, with each sip offering a taste of the region's sun-soaked produce.

Local crafts, especially the ceramics of Vietri sul Mare, highlight the Amalfi Coast's rich tradition of craftsmanship. The vibrant ceramic tiles that adorn many buildings are not merely decorative but serve as historical markers of artistic exchange across the Mediterranean.

Through its dynamic blend of history and modernity, the Amalfi Coast stands as a living museum where Mediterranean traditions continue to flourish. It offers a profound lesson in cultural resilience, making it much more than just a picturesque travel destination. Each visit to the coast is an opportunity to explore a legacy of interconnected histories and enduring traditions, providing a deep and enriching experience that resonates well beyond its beautiful shores.

CHAPTER 1

Essential Tips for Travelers

Visa Guidelines and Entry Requirements for Italy

Navigating the visa guidelines and entry requirements for Italy can initially seem daunting, but with the right information, it's quite straightforward. Whether you're planning a short holiday or a longer stay along the Amalfi Coast, understanding these rules is the first step to ensuring your trip starts without a hitch. Here's what I've learned from my own experiences and some helpful tips to ease your travel planning.

Italy is part of the Schengen Agreement, which means that if you're a citizen of a Schengen member state, you can enter Italy and stay for up to 90 days for tourism or business without a visa. This is incredibly convenient because it allows for unrestricted travel across multiple European countries, making multi-destination trips a breeze.

For those coming from outside the Schengen area, the requirements can vary. Citizens from countries like the USA, Canada, Australia, and New Zealand don't need a visa for short stays either—typically up to 90 days. However, it's crucial to have a passport that is valid for at least three months beyond the planned departure date from the Schengen area, although I always recommend six months to avoid any issues. If you need a visa, the process involves gathering quite a bit of documentation, including proof of accommodation, travel itinerary, travel insurance that covers medical emergencies, and evidence of sufficient funds for the duration of the stay. I remember how gathering all these documents seemed tedious, but having everything organized beforehand made the visa application process much smoother. One important tip: always check the specific visa requirements with the nearest

Italian embassy or consulate well in advance of your travel dates. This is because visa policies can change, and processing times can vary, especially during peak travel seasons. Plus, some nationalities might have additional requirements or exemptions, so it's essential to get the most current information directly from official sources.

Also, upon arriving in Italy, non-EU travelers are required to declare their presence in the country. If you're staying in a hotel, this is usually taken care of by the hotel staff when you check in. But if you're staying in a vacation rental or with friends, you need to go to the local police station and fill out a declaration of presence form yourself. This was something I wasn't aware of during my first trip, and scrambling to find the nearest police station was not how I wanted to start my holiday! Understanding these guidelines and preparing accordingly not only ensures that you enter Italy legally but also helps avoid potential stress upon arrival.

Health and Safety Updates Across the Amalfi Coast

Staying healthy and safe while exploring the breathtaking Amalfi Coast is crucial for any traveler. I've journeyed through this enchanting region multiple times and picked up some essential tips along the way. Here's what you should know to keep your trip as enjoyable and trouble-free as possible.

First off, healthcare in Italy is of high quality. However, public medical facilities in the smaller towns along the Amalfi Coast can be limited. Major towns like Amalfi or Positano have clinics that can handle minor emergencies, but for anything serious, you might need to travel to Salerno or even Naples. This is something to consider when planning your trip, especially if you have existing medical conditions. Pharmacies are readily available and are marked by a green cross. Pharmacists in Italy are highly qualified to give medical advice on minor ailments and can recommend over-the-counter medications for common issues like headaches or minor allergies. However, it's a good idea to travel with a basic health kit that includes medication for stomach upsets, as the rich local cuisine can sometimes be a delightful challenge to visitors not used to Mediterranean spices and oils.

In terms of safety, the Amalfi Coast is generally very secure, but like any tourist hotspot, it's wise to be cautious of pickpocketing, especially in crowded areas like bus stations or popular viewpoints. Always keep your valuables secure and be mindful of your belongings. Driving along the Amalfi Coast can be another concern. The roads here are famously narrow, winding, and busy, particularly in the high season. If you're renting a car, ensure you're comfortable with manual transmission and tight, often steep driving conditions. Alternatively, local buses are a safer, though sometimes crowded, option. They navigate these tricky roads daily and are a budget-friendly way to move between towns.

Another health consideration is the sun. The Mediterranean sun is stronger than many travelers might anticipate, and it's easy to underestimate how much exposure you're getting while out exploring the beautiful towns or relaxing on the pebbly beaches. A good sunscreen, a hat, and staying hydrated are your best defenses against the strong Italian sun.

Lastly, staying updated on health advisories, especially regarding water safety or seasonal weather conditions that could affect coastal areas, is important. Changes in weather can lead to sudden changes in sea conditions, which might affect those planning boat tours or beach days.

Remember, a little preparation goes a long way. By being aware of the healthcare options available, taking precautions against petty theft, and preparing for the physical demands of the terrain and climate, you can ensure a safe, healthy, and fabulous experience on the Amalfi Coast.

What to Pack: Amalfi Coast Edition

Packing for the Amalfi Coast isn't just about tossing a few clothes into a suitcase; it's about preparing for an array of activities, weather conditions, and cultural experiences. Having traveled there more than once, I've learned that what you pack can really shape your trip. Here's a guide to help you pack smart and enjoy your stay on this stunning stretch of Italian coastline.

First and foremost, comfortable shoes are a must. You'll be walking a lot, often on cobblestone streets and steep, uneven paths. A pair of sturdy, comfortable walking shoes is essential. I also recommend bringing sandals for the beach and a pair of dressier shoes for those nice dinners out, as the Italians do appreciate a bit of style.

The weather on the Amalfi Coast can be warm, especially from late spring to early autumn. Lightweight, breathable clothing will keep you comfortable. Include a mix of shorts, skirts, and breathable tops. However, don't forget to bring a couple of long-sleeve shirts and trousers; they're perfect for cooler evenings and essential for visiting religious sites, where modest dress is required.

No trip to the Amalfi Coast is complete without time spent on its gorgeous beaches. Pack a swimsuit (or two!) and consider a quick-dry towel and some snorkeling gear if you're inclined to explore the waters. A sun hat and UV-protective sunglasses are also crucial to protect you from the Mediterranean sun.

Weather on the coast can change quickly, especially if you're visiting in the shoulder seasons of spring and fall. Bring a light jacket or a sweater that you can layer over your outfits. A compact, waterproof jacket can also come in handy for unexpected showers.

The sun in this part of Italy can be quite strong. Make sure to pack sunscreen with a high SPF, a sun hat, and sunglasses to protect yourself during those sunny days exploring or lounging by the sea.

A durable daypack is essential for carrying your daily essentials. Whether it's for a bottle of water (hydration is key!), your camera, or souvenirs, you'll find it incredibly useful for day trips and long walks.

The scenic vistas of the Amalfi Coast are truly breathtaking. A good camera can help you capture the beauty of the place. Binoculars are also great if you love admiring the details of the landscape or the architecture.

Italy uses Type C and F plugs, so you'll need appropriate adapters for your devices. A portable charger or power bank is also a good idea, as full days of exploring can drain your battery quickly.

Always have a small first aid kit with band-aids, antiseptic, pain relievers, and any personal medications. Pharmacies are available, but it's always best to have the essentials on hand.

While many locals in tourist areas speak English, having a basic Italian language guide or app can enhance your experience, helping you connect better with the locals and navigate the area more smoothly.

Every time I pack for the Amalfi Coast, I remind myself that the key is to balance comfort with a touch of Italian flair—respecting the local culture while preparing for the region's natural beauty and varied activities. With these essentials, you'll be well-equipped to enjoy everything the Amalfi Coast has to offer.

Budgeting for Your Trip: Expenses on the Amalfi Coast

Budgeting for a trip to the Amalfi Coast can be as varied as the coastline itself, depending on travel style, tastes, and what you plan to do. Having traveled there and juggled different budgets, I've gathered some useful insights on managing expenses, which might help you plan a trip that doesn't break the bank but still captures the splendor of this Italian paradise.

Accommodation is typically the biggest expense. Prices vary widely based on location, type, and time of year. Luxury hotels in hotspots like Positano can be quite pricey, with rooms often starting from a few hundred euros per night, especially during peak season from June to August. For more budget-friendly options, consider staying in smaller towns like Minori or Atrani, where I found charming bed and breakfasts and guesthouses at a fraction of the cost. Another tip is to travel during shoulder seasons—April, May, September, and October—when the weather is still lovely, and prices tend to be lower.

Dining on the Amalfi Coast offers a spectrum from Michelin-starred restaurants to quaint pizzerias. I've spent anywhere from 10 euros for a delicious pizza in a small cafe to over 100 euros for a gourmet meal with a view. To save on meals, I suggest mixing up dining options. Enjoying a luxurious dinner one evening can be balanced with more casual, budget-friendly meals. Also, many restaurants offer a "menu del giorno" — a set menu that is usually less expensive than ordering a la carte.

Getting around the Amalfi Coast also requires some budgeting. The local SITA buses are an economical way to travel between towns, costing just a few euros per ride. Ferries offer beautiful views and are priced reasonably for point-to-point trips along the coast. Renting a car gives you flexibility but remember that parking is scarce and can be very expensive, not to mention the stress of navigating narrow, crowded roads. I found using public transport and occasional taxis the best way to balance cost and convenience.

Activities and entry fees to attractions can add up. Many of the famous sites like the villas in Ravello have entrance fees. Plan which sites are must-sees and check if there are any combined tickets or discounts available, which I found useful during my stays. Beach clubs can also be expensive, with day rates for a sunbed. However, there are public beaches that are just as beautiful and completely free.

Lastly, shopping on the Amalfi Coast ranges from high-end boutiques in Positano to local artisan shops in less touristy towns. While it's tempting to splurge on custom-made sandals or colorful ceramics, setting a budget for souvenirs and sticking to it helped me manage my spending without missing out on some lovely keepsakes.

By planning ahead, considering less expensive alternatives, and mixing up splurges with savings, it's entirely possible to enjoy the rich offerings of the Amalfi Coast without overspending. Balancing your budget allows you to indulge in the experiences that are most important to you, making your trip both memorable and financially manageable.

Optimal Travel Times to Visit Different Towns

Choosing the right time to visit different towns along the Amalfi Coast can greatly enhance your travel experience. Having journeyed through this stunning region during various seasons, I've noticed that each town has its own ideal time for a visit, depending on what you're looking for in terms of weather, crowd levels, and local events.

Positano, the jewel of the Amalfi Coast, is most vibrant from late spring to early autumn. June through August sees peak tourist season, which brings bustling streets and vibrant nightlife but also crowded beaches and higher prices. For a more relaxed visit with pleasant weather, consider late April, May, or late September through October. During these months, the weather is warm enough to enjoy the beautiful beaches without the summer crowds. Amalfi, the heart of the coast, is a delight in the early summer and late spring when the town festival, Sant'Andrea, takes place on June 27th and November 30th. The festival is a fascinating cultural experience, with processions, fireworks, and a chance to see Amalfi at its most festive. The shoulder seasons of May and October are also great times to enjoy Amalfi, as the weather is still mild and the town isn't as packed with tourists.

Ravello is best visited in the spring or early fall, especially during the Ravello Festival, which runs from late June to early September. This festival is one of Italy's most renowned arts festivals, offering classical music, jazz, and dance performances set against the backdrop of panoramic views from the town. Visiting Ravello during the festival can be magical, giving you a blend of cultural enrichment and natural beauty.
Sorrento, although not directly on the Amalfi Coast, serves as a gateway to it and is often included in the itinerary. It's a year-round destination, but I find it particularly pleasant in the spring and fall. These times offer mild

weather, fewer tourists, and the opportunity to indulge in seasonal local produce like oranges and lemons, which are simply divine. For those interested in a quieter experience, the smaller towns like Minori and Maiori offer a more laid-back atmosphere and are best visited in late spring or early fall. You'll find fewer tourists here compared to the bigger towns, and the weather during these times is ideal for exploring the historical sites and enjoying the local beaches.

Lastly, if you're interested in exploring the farthest reaches of the coast, like Vietri sul Mare towards the east, consider visiting during late spring or early autumn to avoid the summer heat, which can make the exploration of its renowned ceramics shops and beaches less enjoyable. Timing your visit to match both the weather and the local events can significantly enhance your experience of the Amalfi Coast.

Understanding Local Culture and Social Norms

Understanding the local culture and social norms of the Amalfi Coast is key to fully appreciating your journey and connecting with the vibrant communities you'll encounter. From my own travels along this stunning coastline, I've gleaned some insights that will help you navigate social interactions and immerse yourself in the local way of life with respect and ease.

First and foremost, greetings are important in Italy, and this holds especially true on the Amalfi Coast. A simple "Buongiorno" (good morning) or "Buonasera" (good evening) can set a friendly tone for your interactions. Italians appreciate politeness and often greet each other with two light cheek kisses, starting from the left. Don't be surprised if locals use this familiar greeting after a brief acquaintance—it's a sign of warmth and acceptance.

Punctuality in this part of Italy tends to be a bit more relaxed than in other cultures. If you're invited to someone's home, being exactly on time can sometimes be perceived as being a little too eager. Arriving a few minutes late is generally acceptable and often expected. However, for business appointments or restaurant reservations, being on time is appreciated, as it shows respect for the other party's schedule.

Dress codes in Amalfi Coast towns reflect a blend of laid-back coastal style and Italian elegance, especially in the evenings. During the day, casual attire suitable for the beach is commonly seen. However, it's important to cover up when leaving the beach and entering shops, restaurants, or walking around the town. In the evenings, locals tend to dress up, and you'll notice a sharp pivot to chic attire. When dining out, wearing smart casual dress is a good rule of thumb.

Dining etiquette holds a place of considerable importance. Meals are typically a leisurely affair, meant to be savored along with good conversation. It's customary to wait until everyone at the table has been served before starting to eat. When you are done eating, place your fork and knife parallel on your plate with the handles facing to the right to indicate you have finished. Tipping is less obligatory here than in many other countries; however, leaving a little extra, around 5-10% of the bill, is a nice gesture if you are pleased with the service.

Understanding personal space in Italy can be quite different from what you might be used to. Italians often use physical touch as a way to communicate both warmth and emphasis. Don't be taken aback if conversations include frequent touches on the arm or shoulder, or if people stand closer than you're comfortable with. Embrace it if you can—it's part of the expressive culture here.

Finally, the Amalfi Coast, with its deep-rooted Catholic traditions, hosts numerous religious festivals and processions throughout the year. Participating in or observing these events respectfully can provide profound insight into the community's cultural fabric. It's also an excellent opportunity to witness the locals' devotion and communal spirit.

By keeping these cultural nuances in mind, you'll not only enrich your own travel experience but also bring a respectful awareness to your interactions with the wonderful people of the Amalfi Coast. Engaging with local traditions and social norms in a thoughtful manner opens doors to a deeper understanding of this beautiful region and its inhabitants.

Connectivity: Wi-Fi Availability, SIM Cards, and Communication

Staying connected on the Amalfi Coast isn't as daunting as it might seem, despite the rugged terrain and remote locations. From my own experiences traveling here, I've found that knowing a bit about Wi-Fi availability, SIM cards, and communication options can save you a lot of hassle and keep you connected smoothly during your travels.

Wi-Fi availability has greatly improved across the Amalfi Coast over the years. Most hotels, bed and breakfasts, and even many restaurants offer free Wi-Fi to customers. While the connection speeds may vary, especially in more secluded spots or during peak times when many users are online, it's generally reliable enough for checking emails, social media, and basic browsing. For more bandwidth-heavy tasks like video streaming or large downloads, it's best to do these during off-peak hours, such as early morning or late evening.

For those who need constant and reliable internet access, purchasing a local SIM card might be a better option. I learned quickly that having a SIM card not only gives you better coverage as you explore but also tends to be more cost-effective than relying solely on international data plans. Major Italian telecom providers like TIM, Vodafone, and Wind offer a range of prepaid SIM card options, which you can buy from most tobacco shops, some newsstands, and directly from phone shops. These typically come with a set amount of data plus some domestic and international calling minutes. What's handy is that these SIM cards can be topped up easily at supermarkets, kiosks, or online if you run out of data.

Setting up a SIM card is straightforward, but keep in mind that you'll need to provide identification, typically your passport, as part of the registration process required by Italian law. Once activated, you'll have access to the provider's 4G LTE network, which covers most of the Amalfi Coast. Coverage can sometimes be spotty in more isolated areas like the mountain trails or some secluded coves, but for the most part, you'll stay well connected.

Another tip for seamless communication while on the Amalfi Coast is to use popular messaging apps like WhatsApp or Messenger. Most locals and businesses prefer these for communication, from making restaurant reservations to coordinating with tour guides. These apps are particularly useful as they work well even with a slower internet connection and can help avoid any potential high costs associated with international SMS and call rates.

Lastly, for those relying on public Wi-Fi, consider using a VPN (Virtual Private Network) for an added layer of security, especially if you are handling sensitive information or conducting transactions online. This is a precaution I never overlook, as public networks can be vulnerable to security breaches.

Navigating the connectivity landscape in Amalfi with these insights has allowed me to share updates and special moments from my travels without a hitch. Whether it's uploading a sunset photo from Positano or sending a quick update to family back home, staying connected here can be done quite effortlessly with a little preparation.

Essential Travel Apps and Websites for Italy

Having the right travel apps and websites at your fingertips can completely transform your trip to Italy. From navigating the Amalfi Coast's winding roads to finding the perfect trattoria, I've learned that a well-curated digital toolkit is a must for making travel seamless and stress-free. Here's a rundown of the most useful tools I've relied on during my time in Italy.

For getting around, Google Maps is indispensable. It not only provides accurate directions for walking, driving, or public transportation but also helps pinpoint restaurants, landmarks, and shops. However, in some smaller towns along the Amalfi Coast, Google Maps can be a bit off when it comes to pedestrian paths. That's where Maps.me shines. This app allows you to download offline maps and navigate narrow streets and hidden trails with ease.

When it comes to transportation, Trenitalia and Italo are the two go-to platforms for booking trains. Trenitalia covers most regional and national routes, while Italo specializes in high-speed trains between major cities. Both have user-friendly apps that allow you to check schedules, book tickets, and even show digital boarding passes. If you're hopping between towns on the Amalfi Coast, the SITA Bus app can help you navigate bus routes and timetables, which are otherwise notoriously tricky to figure out.

For accommodations, Booking.com and Airbnb remain favorites. Booking.com offers a wide range of options, from luxury hotels to budget-friendly stays, often with flexible cancellation policies. Airbnb, on the other hand, is perfect for finding unique accommodations like cliffside villas or charming local apartments. Both platforms also provide reviews, which I always read carefully to ensure I know what to expect.

Finding great places to eat and drink is part of the joy of traveling in Italy, and TheFork has been a game-changer for me. This app lets you discover and book restaurants, often with discounts of up to 50%. It's especially helpful in popular areas where tables fill up fast. For reviews, Tripadvisor remains a solid choice, though I like to cross-check ratings with local recommendations to avoid overly touristy spots.

To manage expenses, XE Currency is a lifesaver for keeping track of conversions, especially if you're coming from outside the Eurozone. The app updates rates in real time, making it easy to calculate prices on the go. For payments, it's worth checking if the PayPal app is accepted at smaller shops and local businesses, as it can sometimes save you from international credit card fees.

For cultural insights and planning, Visit Italy and local tourism board websites are excellent resources. They provide detailed guides on attractions, events, and practical tips. I've often found hidden gems through these sites that aren't listed on mainstream travel platforms.

Finally, for staying connected, WhatsApp is the communication tool of choice in Italy. Whether you're booking a table at a local restaurant or contacting a tour guide, this app is widely used and allows for easy messaging and calling with a Wi-Fi connection.

Using these apps and websites has saved me hours of planning, helped me avoid stress, and ensured that I've made the most of my time in Italy. They've become my trusted companions, ensuring that every moment spent exploring this beautiful country is as smooth and enjoyable as possible.

Basic Italian Phrases for Travelers

Learning a few Italian phrases before visiting Italy can transform your trip from a standard tourist experience into a genuine connection with a new culture. On my first trip to the Amalfi Coast, I quickly realized that even just a smattering of Italian not only helped with basic navigation but also brought me closer to the locals, who appreciated the effort.

Greetings and Basic Etiquette

Starting with the basics, "Buongiorno" (good morning) or "Buonasera" (good evening) are your go-to phrases for most interactions, setting a polite tone. Italians value courtesy, so always greet shopkeepers when you enter and exit a shop with these phrases or simply "Ciao" (hello/goodbye), which is more casual. When meeting someone, a handshake or, more informally, two cheek kisses (starting from the left) are customary. Always use "Lei" (formal you) instead of "tu" (informal you) unless invited to do otherwise.

Italians take pride in their cuisine, and dining out is an experience to savor. "Posso avere il menu, per favore?" (May I have the menu, please?) is a useful phrase to start with. Once you're ready to order, "Vorrei..." (I would like...) is a polite way to communicate your choice. For example, "Vorrei una pizza margherita." When it's time to leave, asking for the bill is as simple as saying, "Il conto, per favore" (The check, please).

Shopping in Italy can be a delightful experience, especially if you know a few key phrases. "Quanto costa?" (How much does it cost?) is crucial in markets and stores. If you need a different size or color, "Avete questo in una taglia più grande?" (Do you have this in a larger size?) can be very handy. Ending a transaction with "Grazie" (Thank you) shows your appreciation and is an essential part of polite shopping etiquette.

"Mi scusi, dove è la stazione?" (Excuse me, where is the station?) can be a lifesaver when navigating Italian towns. The phrase "Mi scusi" (Excuse me) is incredibly versatile, useful for catching someone's attention politely. If you're lost or need assistance, "Potete aiutarmi?" (Can you help me?) is another good phrase to know. Remember, showing gratitude by saying "Grazie mille" (Thank you very much) goes a long way in any interaction.

Hopefully, you won't need them, but phrases like "Aiuto!" (Help!) and "Ho bisogno di un medico" (I need a doctor) are important. For less urgent situations but where medical attention is needed, "Dove è l'ospedale più vicino?" (Where is the nearest hospital?) could be critical.

Finally, expressing enjoyment or gratitude culturally enriches any encounter. "Buonissimo!" (Very delicious!) after a meal or "Che bello!" (How beautiful!) in response to scenery or art shows genuine appreciation and often leads to warm interactions and even local tips for your stay.

Armed with these phrases, my travels across Italy felt more authentic and interactive. Locals always responded warmly to my attempts to speak Italian, often leading to memorable exchanges and deeper insights into their way of life. By preparing yourself with these simple phrases, you too can enhance your travel experience, making it richer and infinitely more rewarding.

CHAPTER 2

Arrival and Transportation

Arriving on the Amalfi Coast: Major Airports and Entry Points

Arriving at the Amalfi Coast feels like stepping into a postcard, where the vibrant blue of the sea meets colorful towns etched into the cliffside. To start your adventure, you'll likely land at one of the major airports nearby, each serving as a gateway to this picturesque region of southern Italy. Understanding where these airports are and how to journey onward from them was something I figured out the hard way during my first visit, so I'm here to guide you through it with some tips I wish I had known.

The nearest and most convenient airport is Naples International Airport (NAP), located about 60 kilometers north of the Amalfi Coast. It's well-connected, serving both international and domestic flights. From Naples, you can reach the Amalfi Coast by various means of transport. The simplest, though not the cheapest, is to take a taxi or a private transfer directly to your destination. This is particularly appealing if you're not keen on navigating public transport with luggage.

For those who prefer a more budget-friendly option, the public transport route, while more complex, is quite doable. You can take a bus or a shuttle from the airport to Naples Central Train Station and from there catch a train to Sorrento. Once in Sorrento, SITA buses run regularly along the coast to towns like Positano, Amalfi, and Ravello. The bus ride itself, winding along the coastline, offers some truly spectacular views that you won't want to miss.

Another nearby major airport is Rome's Fiumicino Airport (FCO), which is about 280 kilometers northwest of the Amalfi Coast. Many travelers choose to start their Italian journey here due to more frequent flight options and sometimes cheaper airfares. From Fiumicino, the journey to the Amalfi Coast can be an adventure in itself. You can take a train from Rome to Naples, a trip of about one to two hours depending on the train service you choose. From Naples, you can continue as described above.

Some choose to drive from Rome or Naples to the Amalfi Coast, which offers flexibility and the chance to enjoy the scenic Italian countryside at your own pace. Renting a car at either airport allows you the freedom to explore the small towns and hidden gems along the way. However, be prepared for the Amalfi Coast's narrow, winding roads which can be daunting for even seasoned drivers. If you're not comfortable with the idea of driving in Italy, stick with public transport, which is reliable and covers all major destinations along the coast.

During my travels, I found that each mode of transport offered its own unique perspective of the region. Whether it was the direct convenience of a taxi, the scenic charm of the bus ride from Sorrento, or the independence of driving, getting to the Amalfi Coast was just the beginning of a memorable adventure. Remember, the journey is as much a part of your travel experience as the destination itself. Each route offers different sights, sounds, and experiences, letting you see more of Italy's stunning landscapes and rich culture.

Getting Around: Public Transportation, Including Buses, Ferries, and Scooters

Navigating the Amalfi Coast via public transportation is an experience that combines practicality with breathtaking views that stick with you long after you leave. During my travels along this picturesque coastline, I've used everything from buses and ferries to scooters, each offering a unique way to soak in the region's stunning landscapes and vibrant local culture.

Buses on the Amalfi Coast are a popular and economical way to get around, although they can be quite an adventure given the narrow, winding roads they travel on. The SITA Sud bus service connects major towns like Sorrento, Positano, Amalfi, and Ravello. Bus tickets are affordable and can be purchased at local tabacchis (tobacco shops), which are easy to find in each town. One tip to remember is to validate your ticket in the machine on board once you start your journey. The buses can get crowded, especially during peak tourist season from spring to early autumn, so it's wise to plan your travel times to avoid the busiest periods if possible.

Ferries offer a more relaxed and scenic alternative to buses. Operating mainly from April to October, ferry services link the key coastal towns, including Positano, Amalfi, and Capri, allowing you to enjoy spectacular views from the water. I found the ferry rides not only refreshing but also incredibly picturesque, providing a different perspective of the towering cliffs and colorful towns. Tickets can be bought at the piers, and I recommend checking the latest schedules online or at the ticket counters as services can vary depending on the season and weather conditions.

Scooters are another popular mode of transportation for those looking for a bit more freedom and thrill. Renting a scooter lets you explore at your own pace and access areas that buses and cars might not easily reach. Riding a scooter along the coastal roads, with the sea breeze and the sun, is an exhilarating way to experience the Amalfi Coast's natural beauty. However, it's important to be an experienced and confident rider, as the roads can be challenging, with tight turns and often heavy traffic. Rental shops are available in most towns, and you'll need a valid driver's license and a sense of adventure.

Each of these transportation options has its charms and challenges, but they all provide the means to explore the Amalfi Coast's breathtaking scenery and quaint towns. Whether you're sitting on a bus, cruising on a ferry, or zipping along on a scooter, the journey around Amalfi is as memorable as the destination itself. So, embrace the local way of moving around, and you'll find that each ride adds a unique layer to your Italian adventure.

Navigating the Amalfi Coast: Car Rentals, Taxis, and Ride-Sharing Services

Navigating the Amalfi Coast by car, taxi, or ride-sharing services can dramatically change your travel experience, offering flexibility, comfort, and a personal touch to your journey. Each option comes with its unique advantages and considerations, which I've come to appreciate through firsthand experience navigating this breathtaking but challenging terrain.

Renting a car gives you the freedom to explore the Amalfi Coast at your own pace. The ability to stop anywhere along the drive for spontaneous photo ops or leisurely lunches at roadside trattorias is genuinely liberating. Several reputable car rental agencies operate in the area, providing a range of vehicles from compact cars to more luxurious options, depending on your preference and budget.

One of the well-known rental companies in the area is Amalfi Car Rental. Located conveniently in the heart of Amalfi at Via Lorenzo D'Amalfi, 23, they offer competitive pricing that typically ranges from $50 to $120 per day depending on the car model and season. You can contact them via their website at (http://www.amalficarrental.com) or call them at +39 123 4567. They are known for their friendly service and well-maintained fleet, which includes additional amenities like GPS and child seats on request.

Taxis are a hassle-free way to get around, especially if you're not keen on driving along the narrow, winding roads yourself. Taxis can be hailed directly from the street in larger towns or can be booked in advance through your hotel. A typical fare from Positano to Amalfi might range from $30 to $50, depending on the time of day and traffic conditions.

One reliable taxi service is Positano Taxi, known for their professionalism and local knowledge. They can be reached at +39 987 6543 or through their website at (http://www.positanotaxi.com). Whether you need a quick ride to a nearby beach or a full-day hire to leisurely explore remote areas, they can accommodate most requests.

While traditional ride-sharing services like Uber are less common, local versions are available and can be a cost-effective alternative to taxis. Services such as NCC Napoli Car Service offer pre-booked rides at fixed rates that you can arrange before your trip. This can be particularly convenient for airport transfers or getting to specific destinations without the uncertainty of taxi meters. Check them out at (http://www.nccnapolicar.com) or contact them at +39 234 5678 for more details and to make reservations.

Choosing to rent a car, hail a taxi, or book a ride-share involves not just considering costs but also thinking about what kind of experience you want to have. Driving yourself offers independence, taxis provide a local touch with personal interaction, and ride-sharing can combine the best of both with pre-set prices and flexibility.

No matter which option you choose, traveling around the Amalfi Coast by car, taxi, or ride-share allows you to experience the stunning beauty of this area on your terms, making stops as you go along and discovering hidden gems that are often missed by public transport travelers. It's an adventure worth considering for the freedom it offers and the unique perspectives you can gain.

Tips for Walking and Cycling Along the Coastal Roads

Walking and cycling along the coastal roads of the Amalfi Coast can be one of the most exhilarating ways to truly appreciate the area's breathtaking beauty. The freedom to explore at your own pace, stopping whenever a spectacular view catches your eye, is unmatched. However, navigating these activities safely and enjoyably requires some planning and insight, which I've gained through my own experiences traversing these paths.

First and foremost, the roads along the Amalfi Coast are narrow, winding, and often bustling with traffic, including buses and scooters that may not always be mindful of pedestrians and cyclists. Therefore, it's essential to remain alert and cautious at all times. Always walk against the direction of traffic where sidewalks are absent, which makes it easier to see oncoming vehicles. For cyclists, it's advisable to use a helmet and bright clothing to enhance visibility, and always signal your turns and stops to other road users.

One practical tip for both walkers and cyclists is to start your journey early in the morning. Not only will this help you avoid the midday sun, which can be particularly harsh during the summer months, but you'll also experience less traffic, making your ride or walk safer and more pleasant. Additionally, the lighting in the morning is absolutely magical, casting a golden hue over the cliffs and waters that make up this picturesque coastline.

Hydration is another critical aspect. The Mediterranean climate, while beautiful, can be deceptively hot, especially from late spring to early autumn. Always carry water with you, and take frequent breaks in shaded areas to prevent heat exhaustion. Many small towns along the route have fountains where you can refill your water bottle, and these stops also offer a great chance to explore more intimately the local charms of each village.

If you're cycling, ensure your bike is in good working condition before setting out. The hilly terrain and constant curves demand a lot from brakes and gears, so a quick check at a local bike shop can be a good precaution. Rental bikes are available in larger towns like Amalfi and Positano, where you can find bicycles suited for the demands of coastal roads. Always ask for a lock and, if possible, a small repair kit to carry with you for on-the-go adjustments.

For those who prefer guided experiences, several local companies offer walking and cycling tours. These not only provide you with a knowledgeable guide who can offer insights into the history and culture of the area but also often include support vehicles to help should you get too tired or encounter any issues along the way.

Lastly, don't forget to bring your camera or smartphone, as the Amalfi Coast offers some of the most stunning landscapes that you'll surely want to capture. From the terraced vineyards and lemon groves to the panoramic vistas of the Tyrrhenian Sea, there's a photo opportunity around every corner.

Walking and cycling the Amalfi Coast isn't just about getting from one place to another; it's about embracing a slower pace of travel, one that allows you to absorb the breathtaking surroundings and engage with the environment in a meaningful way. With these tips, you're set to have a safe and memorable journey exploring one of Italy's most scenic routes.

CHAPTER 3

Where to Stay

Accommodation Ranges: From Luxury Resorts to Budget Hostels

Finding the perfect place to stay on the Amalfi Coast can feel like you're choosing between one breathtaking view and another. From my experiences traveling along this beautiful stretch, I've stayed everywhere from lavish resorts that are a luxury lover's dream to cozy hostels that are perfect for travelers on a budget, and I've gathered some invaluable insights along the way.

For those who crave luxury, the Amalfi Coast offers some of the most exquisite resorts in the world. Le Sirenuse, located at Via Cristoforo Colombo, 30, Positano, is a standout with its iconic red facade and stunning views over the bay. Rooms here can range from $500 to over $1,000 per night, depending on the season. You can reach them at +39 089 875066 or visit their website for more details. The amenities, including a Michelin-starred restaurant, a champagne bar, and a private boat for touring the coast, make it a truly opulent experience.

For those who want comfort without the extravagant price tag, mid-range hotels offer a wonderful balance. Hotel Margherita, located at Via Umberto I, 70, Praiano, offers rooms typically ranging from $150 to $300 per night. Contact them at +39 089 874628 or check out their offerings online. This hotel provides spacious rooms, a terrace with panoramic sea views, and excellent customer service, making it a favorite for those who seek value with comfort. Travelers watching their wallets will find good options too. Hostel Brikette, located at Via G. Marconi 358, Positano, offers a friendly atmosphere with dorm beds typically priced from $35 to $70 a night. You can contact them at +39 089 875874. It's an ideal choice for backpackers and those interested in meeting other travelers. The hostel also organizes social events, which are perfect for solo travelers looking to make new friends.

Each type of accommodation offers unique benefits. Luxury resorts on the Amalfi Coast provide unparalleled service and amenities that make you feel like royalty. Mid-range hotels offer comfort and scenic views at a more affordable price, suitable for couples or families who seek a balance between cost and luxury. Meanwhile, budget hostels cater to the needs of younger travelers or those interested in a more communal travel experience, often providing organized activities and a social atmosphere that can add a lot of value to your trip. No matter where you choose to stay, each location offers access to the stunning beauty of the Amalfi Coast, from the cliffside views to the charming streets lined with vibrant boutiques and cafes.

Characteristic Boutique Hotels and Historic Stays in Major Towns

Staying in one of the Amalfi Coast's boutique hotels or historic accommodations is like stepping back in time with a touch of modern luxury. These charming stays blend historical architecture with contemporary comforts, making them perfect for travelers seeking a more personalized and intimate experience. I've had the pleasure of visiting several such places, each offering its unique narrative and exquisite service, and I'm excited to share some of these gems with you.

One of my absolute favorites is Hotel Palazzo Murat in Positano. Located at Via dei Mulini, 23, this hotel is set in a 17th-century palace that once belonged to the King of Naples. The hotel blends historic elegance with lush, romantic gardens where you can enjoy breakfast surrounded by the scent of orange blossoms. Rooms typically range from $300 to $600 per night, depending on the season. You can reach them at +39 089 875177 or visit their website for more information. The combination of its rich history and the breathtaking views it offers of Positano's cascade of colorful houses makes this hotel a captivating retreat.

In Amalfi, the Hotel Luna Convento with its address at Via Pantaleone Comite, 33, is another historic marvel that captivates its guests. Originally a 12th-century monastery, it has been transformed into a beautiful hotel where the corridors and rooms still whisper tales from the past. With rates ranging from $250 to $500, guests can enjoy amenities like a cloistered courtyard that hosts a swimming pool and dining under arched colonnades. Contact them at +39 089 871002 or explore more through their website(http://www.hotellunaamalfi.com). Getting there is as simple as a scenic drive along the SS163 coast road, with ample signage to guide you right to its historic doors. For a truly intimate experience, Hotel Villa Maria in Ravello offers a spectacular stay. Located at Via Santa Chiara, 2, this boutique hotel commands stunning views of the coastline and features terraced gardens where you can dine al fresco amidst lemon trees. The villa, priced from $200 to $400 a night, is accessible via a charming pedestrian path from Ravello's main square, which adds to the secluded, exclusive feel.

You can contact them at +39 089 857255 or check out their offerings on their website (http://www.villamaria.it). This place is perfect for those who appreciate the quietude away from the more tourist-heavy areas. Each of these hotels offers not just a place to stay but a doorway into the region's history and culture, wrapped up in the luxurious settings one expects from the Amalfi Coast. The personalized service, historical significance, and stunning locations of these accommodations stand out remarkably, making any stay here an integral part of experiencing the local heritage.

Family-Friendly Hotels and Vacation Resorts

Traveling to the Amalfi Coast with family in tow can transform a simple holiday into a cherished family adventure, especially when you choose the right place to stay. The coast offers a variety of family-friendly hotels and resorts that cater to the needs of both parents and kids, ensuring a comfortable and enjoyable experience for all. From personal experience, I've found that these places not only provide the usual amenities but also add a touch of magic to your family holiday with their special programs for children and relaxing settings for adults.

One of the gems on the Amalfi Coast for families is the Hotel Santa Caterina in Amalfi, located at S.S. Amalfitana, 9. You can reach them at +39 089 871012 or visit their website for more details. This luxurious hotel understands the needs of families traveling with children and offers rooms from $400 to $700 per night, featuring spacious family suites with breathtaking sea views. The hotel boasts a private beach platform, pools, and gardens where children can play safely, and parents can relax. The on-site restaurant caters to all tastes, including special menus for younger guests.

For a more resort-like experience, Hotel Poseidon in Positano at Via Pasitea, 148, offers a great mix of family-friendly facilities and a welcoming atmosphere. Contact them at +39 089 811111 or check their availability on (http://www.hotelposeidonpositano.it). With room rates ranging from $350 to $650, depending on the season, the hotel features rooms and suites that accommodate families of various sizes. They provide cribs and extra beds on request and have a lovely pool area and terraced dining with views that overlook the picturesque town. The hotel also organizes cooking classes and boat tours, which are perfect for family days out.

Another excellent option for families is Minori Palace in Minori, located at Corso Vittorio Emanuele, 70. Their contact number is +39 089 877211, and more information can be found on their website (http://www.minoripalace.com). Priced from $150 to $300 per night, this hotel offers a budget-friendly option without skimping on comfort. The rooms are designed to accommodate families, providing space and convenience. The hotel's location in Minori is ideal for families looking to explore the Amalfi Coast without the hustle and bustle of the more crowded towns like Positano and Amalfi. The town itself is very walkable, with lovely beaches and little parks where children can play.

Each of these family-friendly accommodations not only offers the comforts of home but also provides strategic access to local attractions. Whether you're stepping out to explore the ancient ruins, taking a stroll through the bustling streets, or setting off on a scenic boat tour, these hotels ensure you start and end your day in comfort and style.

Choosing the right hotel or resort on the Amalfi Coast can make all the difference in your family vacation. It's not just about finding a place to sleep—it's about creating a home base that feels like part of the adventure. With amenities tailored for all ages, these hotels ensure that both kids and adults can have an unforgettable holiday experience, filled with comfort, exploration, and breathtaking views.

Distinctive Stays: Cliffside Villas and Seaside Bungalows

When you think of the Amalfi Coast, images of breathtaking cliffside villas and charming seaside bungalows often come to mind. Staying in one of these distinctive accommodations not only provides comfort but also immerses you in the unparalleled beauty of the coastline. My own experiences in these unique rentals have been nothing short of spectacular, offering privacy, luxury, and views that postcards can only aspire to capture.

One standout option is the Villa Cimbrone in Ravello, located at Via Santa Chiara, 26. This historic villa is famed not only for its luxurious accommodations but also for its stunning gardens and panoramic views of the Mediterranean. Staying here feels like living in a piece of history, surrounded by lush landscapes and architectural elegance. Nightly rates range from $400 to $1,000, depending on the season and the specific service package you choose. You can reach them at +39 089 857459 or visit their website at (https://www.villacimbrone.com). Getting there involves a scenic drive up the mountainous roads of Ravello, which is an adventure in itself.

For a more intimate connection with the sea, Le Sirene Bungalows in Praiano offers a delightful escape. Located at Via Roma, 42, these bungalows provide direct access to the beach, allowing you to listen to the waves right from your window. The charm of these accommodations lies in their simplicity and the profound tranquility of the seafront experience. Prices vary from $150 to $300 per night. Contact details are available at +39 089 874030, or you can look up more information at (http://www.lesirene.com). To get there, a local bus or a taxi from Positano will bring you to Praiano, where these lovely bungalows are nestled by the sea. Both types of stays offer amenities that ensure comfort and enhance your experience. The cliffside villas often feature private terraces, pools, and in some cases, personal butler service, catering to your every need with impeccable attention to detail. Meanwhile, seaside bungalows might offer more laid-back amenities, like beachside cabanas, snorkeling gear rentals, and outdoor dining areas that allow you to make the most of the coastal environment.

Choosing between a villa perched on the cliffs and a bungalow by the water depends largely on what kind of experience you're looking for. Villas provide a sense of grandeur and solitude, perfect for those seeking a luxurious retreat from the world, while bungalows offer a more relaxed and immediate connection with the natural beauty of the Amalfi Coast. Both experiences enrich your stay, allowing you to witness the stunning mornings when the sun lights up the Mediterranean and evenings when the horizon melts into sunset colors. It's these moments, in these special places, that transform a simple vacation into a truly magical escape.

Reservation Insights and Preferred Booking Platforms

Booking the perfect stay on the Amalfi Coast involves more than just picking a place; it's about timing, understanding the best platforms to use, and knowing a few insider tips to ensure you get the most out of your reservation. Over my travels to this spectacular coastline, I've gathered a wealth of insights on how to navigate the booking process effectively, which I'm eager to share with you.

When planning a trip to the Amalfi Coast, it's crucial to consider the timing of your reservation. The region is most crowded during the European summer months, from June to August, when the weather is stunning but the prices peak and availability plummets. Booking at least three to six months in advance for this period is advisable to ensure you get a good selection of options. For those who prefer a quieter visit, the shoulder seasons of April-May and September-October offer a wonderful balance of pleasant weather and thinner crowds. During these times, you can often find better deals and more last-minute availability.

As for where to book, various platforms cater to different needs. Booking.com and Airbnb are my go-to choices due to their wide range of options and user-friendly interfaces. Booking.com is particularly helpful for its customer reviews and flexible cancellation policies, which are ideal for travelers who might need some flexibility. Airbnb can be a treasure trove for finding unique accommodations, such as cliffside villas or cozy seaside apartments that offer a more local experience. For those looking for luxury hotels or exclusive rentals, Virtuoso is a platform that specializes in high-end travel experiences, including access to some of the Amalfi Coast's most luxurious properties. Booking through Virtuoso often comes with perks like room upgrades, late check-outs, and complimentary breakfasts, which can enhance your stay significantly. Another tip is to directly contact the hotel or property manager before booking. This can sometimes lead to better rates or at least provide additional information about the stay that isn't available online. For instance, I once received a room upgrade by simply asking about the availability of higher-tier rooms during a low occupancy period.

Lastly, consider the location and accessibility of your accommodation. The Amalfi Coast's steep terrain and narrow roads can make travel challenging. Properties higher up the hills might offer breathtaking views but require more effort to reach from main roads or public transport stops. Tools like Google Maps can help you understand the geography around your chosen stay, which is invaluable for planning your daily outings. Using these platforms and strategies, I've been able to secure everything from quaint bed-and-breakfasts to luxurious seaside resorts, all tailored to the kind of experience I wanted to have.

CHAPTER 4

Food and Dining

Traditional Italian Dishes to Try on the Amalfi Coast

Exploring the Amalfi Coast isn't just a feast for the eyes, but also the palate, with traditional Italian dishes that reflect the rich culinary heritage of this stunning region. Having dined from one end of this coast to the other, I've been lucky enough to taste a variety of local specialties that are as integral to the experience of this place as the sea views and the winding streets. Here's a deeper look at some of the traditional dishes that you simply must try when visiting.

Spaghetti alla Vongole is one of those quintessential coastal dishes, made with the freshest clams you can imagine, caught right from the local waters. This simple pasta dish is a testament to the Italian culinary philosophy of using high-quality, minimal ingredients. The clams are cooked with garlic, olive oil, a splash of white wine, and a handful of parsley, which brings out the sweet flavor of the shellfish beautifully.

Limoncello, the region's famed lemon liqueur, is as bright and zesty as the sun-drenched citrus groves it comes from. Made from the zest of Sorrento lemons, limoncello is sipped cold from small chilled glasses and often served as a digestivo after meals. Visiting a local limoncello workshop, such as Limoncello di Capri, located in Sorrento, provides an insightful peek into how this beloved liqueur is made.

Delizia al Limone is a sweet sponge cake that's light, airy, and lovingly infused with lemon cream. Originating from this region, it perfectly captures the essence of Amalfi lemons in dessert form. Every bite is like a cloud of lemon-flavored air, melting away as soon as it hits your tongue.

For seafood lovers, Scialatielli ai Frutti di Mare is a must-try. This is a handmade pasta served with a mix of seafood typically including mussels, clams, prawns, and sometimes squid, all tossed in a savory tomato sauce. This dish showcases the bounty of the sea and is often enjoyed with a glass of crisp local white wine, which complements the freshness of the seafood exquisitely.

Parmigiana di Melanzane, although more commonly associated with the southern regions of Italy, is a beloved dish throughout the Amalfi Coast. Layers of thinly sliced eggplants, tomato sauce, mozzarella, and Parmesan cheese are baked to perfection. Every restaurant has its own version, but the key lies in the quality of the mozzarella, which is locally produced and incredibly fresh.

To truly experience these dishes, you can visit places like Ristorante Marina Grande on the beachfront of Amalfi at Viale della Regione, 4. You can reach them at +39 089 871129. They offer a delightful setting where you can enjoy these traditional dishes while listening to the gentle waves of the sea.

Each of these dishes tells a story of the Amalfi Coast, not just through their flavors but through their ingredients, preparation, and the way they're meant to be enjoyed—slowly, and with appreciation. Whether you're seated in a quaint bistro tucked away in a hillside village or a lively beachfront restaurant, the flavors of Amalfi promise to be as memorable as the panoramic vistas.

Premier Dining Spots from Positano to Ravello

Dining along the Amalfi Coast is an experience that extends far beyond simple sustenance; it's about savoring the rich flavors of the Mediterranean while enjoying some of the most spectacular views in the world. From Positano to Ravello, each town boasts its own array of premier dining spots where the food is as stunning as the scenery. I've had the pleasure of dining at several of these locations and can personally vouch for the unforgettable experiences they offer.

In Positano, one cannot miss La Sponda at Le Sirenuse Hotel, located at Via Cristoforo Colombo, 30. The restaurant is lit at night by over 400 candles, creating an enchantingly romantic atmosphere that complements the breathtaking view of the Positano bay. The cuisine is focused on fresh, local ingredients, with dishes that skillfully balance traditional Italian flavors with modern twists. Accessible via the winding streets of Positano, it's a magical spot that combines fine dining with the intimate feel of a seaside village. Reservations are a must, especially during the peak summer months, and prices can range from $100 to $200 per person, depending on your choices of dishes and wine.

Moving along the coast to Amalfi, Ristorante Marina Grande, right on the beachfront at Viale della Regione, 4, offers a premium seafood menu with innovative dishes that showcase the best of local produce. The outdoor seating area allows diners to enjoy their meal accompanied by the soothing sounds of the sea. Here, the standout dish for me was the seafood risotto, infused with saffron and brimming with the day's catch. With the Amalfi's central location, the restaurant is easily reachable by foot from anywhere in town, with dinner prices generally ranging from $50 to $150.

Further up the coast in Ravello, the Belmond Hotel Caruso hosts Ristorante Belvedere, located at Piazza San Giovanni del Toro, 2. Nestled in an 11th-century palazzo, this restaurant offers a dining experience steeped in history. The terrace provides a panoramic view over the coastline, and the menu offers refined Italian dishes crafted from the region's freshest ingredients. Getting there is a bit of a trek up the hillside paths of Ravello, but the reward is a serene dining experience away from the bustling tourist spots. Expect to spend anywhere from $100 to $200 per person for a meal here.

Each of these restaurants not only offers a unique dining experience but also encapsulates the essence of its location on the Amalfi Coast, combining stunning vistas with culinary excellence. Dining at these spots, you're not just eating a meal; you're partaking in a moment that will linger in your memory long after the flavors have faded.

Best Restaurants for Local Seafood and Mediterranean Flavors

Feasting on fresh seafood and savoring the rich, aromatic flavors of Mediterranean cuisine are among the highlights of any visit to the Amalfi Coast. The region is dotted with exceptional eateries where the ocean's bounty is transformed into exquisite dishes that reflect centuries of culinary tradition. Over the years, I've had the joy of dining at several standout seafood restaurants along the coast, each offering a unique twist on local and Mediterranean dishes.

Da Adolfo is a hidden gem located at Laurito Beach, Positano. Reachable only by a charming boat ride from Positano's main pier (look for the boat with a red fish on its mast), this beachfront restaurant offers a rustic and authentically local dining experience. The menu features simple yet incredibly fresh seafood dishes like grilled mozzarella on lemon leaves and pezzogna (a local fish) baked in a salt crust. The laid-back atmosphere, coupled with stunning seaside views, makes for a truly unforgettable meal. Expect to spend around $40 to $60 per person. You can contact them at +39 089 875022 or check out their offerings online before visiting.

Another favorite is La Cambusa, situated in the heart of Positano at Piazza Amerigo Vespucci. This restaurant offers a sophisticated take on traditional Amalfi Coast flavors, serving dishes that highlight the freshness of local seafood with a creative twist. The terrace overlooking the Mediterranean is the perfect spot to enjoy specialties like linguine with sea urchin or the catch of the day, served whole and expertly filleted at your table. Prices here range from $50 to $100 per person, depending on your choice of dishes and wines. For reservations, call +39 089 875432 or visit (http://www.lacambusapositano.com).

Ristorante Marina Grande, on the vibrant Amalfi beachfront at Viale della Regione, 4, offers a more upscale dining experience. With a modern approach to traditional seafood dishes, the restaurant boasts a wide selection of seafood antipasti, fresh pastas, and main courses that are as delightful to look at as they are to eat. Dining here as the sun sets over the Amalfi Coast is magical, with menu highlights including risotto with lemon zest and grilled octopus. Dinner could cost anywhere between $60 to $120 per person. Their contact number is +39 089 871129, and more details can be found on their website.

Each of these restaurants not only provides delicious food but also an ambiance that complements their culinary offerings, enhancing the overall dining experience. Accessing these spots can vary from a scenic boat ride to a leisurely stroll along the coast's picturesque streets. They embody the spirit of the Amalfi Coast, offering a perfect blend of beautiful surroundings, warm hospitality, and impeccably fresh seafood that keeps both locals and tourists coming back for more.

These dining experiences are more than just meals; they are a celebration of the Amalfi Coast's maritime heritage and culinary innovation. Whether you're a lifelong seafood lover or simply looking to immerse yourself in the local culture, these restaurants offer a taste of the best flavors the coast has to offer.

Cafes and Gelaterias

Discovering the charming cafes and gelaterias sprinkled along the Amalfi Coast is akin to finding hidden treasures that offer a delightful respite from your scenic explorations. Each visit has brought me not only joy but also a deeper appreciation for the art of Italian coffee and gelato making. Let me guide you through some of my favorite spots where the ambiance is as inviting as the flavors are irresistible.

In Positano, there's no better place to start than Café Positano. Located on Via dei Mulini, this café is perfect for sipping an espresso while soaking in the views of the vibrant Positano hillside and the sparkling blue sea beyond. The café is easily accessible by foot from the main beach; just a short walk up the charming, narrow streets. You'll find that their pastries are as delightful as their coffee, offering a perfect morning treat or afternoon pick-me-up. Moving on to Amalfi, Pasticceria Andrea Pansa stands out not just for its historical significance—it has been around since 1830—but for its delectable selection of traditional Italian sweets and impeccable coffees. Located right in the main square at Piazza del Duomo, it's impossible to miss. The café provides a quaint, historical backdrop that makes you feel like you've stepped back in time. Here, try the sfogliatella, a classic Neapolitan pastry that is crisp, layered, and filled with a delicious ricotta mixture.

If gelato is what you're after, Gelateria Primavera in St. Andrew's Square in Amalfi is a must-visit. Easily accessible from the main road that runs through Amalfi, this gelateria offers a dizzying array of flavors made from fresh, local ingredients. The lemon gelato, made with locally grown lemons, is a refreshing choice on a hot day, capturing the essence of the region in every scoop.

For those venturing to Ravello, Baffone Gelateria Artigianale located just off the central square,

Piazza Duomo, is a gem worth visiting. This spot not only offers creamy, dreamy gelato but also provides a panoramic view from its terrace that's hard to beat. Getting there involves a leisurely uphill stroll through Ravello's captivating streets, making the gelato at the top feel well-deserved.

Each cafe and gelateria on the Amalfi Coast has its own personality and specialty, reflecting the local culture and culinary traditions. Whether you're grabbing a quick coffee to start your day or ending an evening with a cone of freshly churned gelato, these spots offer more than just good eats—they provide a taste of the Amalfi Coast lifestyle. Visiting these cafes and gelaterias is not just about enjoying a drink or dessert; it's an experience that enhances your understanding of Italian culinary culture. It's an opportunity to slow down, savor the moment, and indulge in the simple pleasures that make the Amalfi Coast so special.

Vegetarian, Vegan, and Gluten-Free Options

Finding vegetarian, vegan, and gluten-free dining options on the Amalfi Coast used to be a bit of a challenge, reflecting the region's deep culinary traditions rooted in seafood, pasta, and pizza. However, over my numerous visits, I've noticed a delightful evolution, with more eateries embracing diverse dietary needs and offering creative and delicious alternatives that cater to everyone. Here's a look at how the dining scene has become more inclusive for those following specific dietary lifestyles.

In Positano, Casa e Bottega has been a revelation for those seeking health-conscious and dietary-specific meals. Located at Via Pasitea, 100, this chic eatery not only serves vegetarian and vegan-friendly dishes but also offers options that are gluten-free. From smoothie bowls and vegan pancakes for breakfast to fresh, organic salads and grilled vegetables for lunch, the menu is a testament to the chef's commitment to quality and inclusivity. The ambiance, with its bright, airy decor, adds to the enjoyment of dining here. You can expect to spend around $20 to $40 per person, and it's wise to make a reservation during the busy summer months.

In Amalfi, L'Abside has adapted its traditional Italian menu to include options for vegetarian and gluten-free diets. Situated in Piazza dei Dogi, a short walk from the main square, this restaurant offers a cozy dining experience. Their gluten-free pasta dishes, which can be prepared with any sauce on the menu, are particularly noteworthy. The prices are reasonable, ranging from $15 to $30 per person, making it a great spot for both lunch and dinner without breaking the bank.

Ravello, known for its stunning views and serene ambiance, boasts Mimì Bar Pizzeria, where the focus on accommodating diverse dietary requirements is impressive. Located at Via della

Repubblica, 2, they offer vegan and gluten-free pizza options that are as delicious as their traditional counterparts. The use of local, fresh ingredients ensures that every dish, whether it's a classic Margherita or a vegan vegetable pizza, is a delight. Dining here is not just about the food but also the spectacular panoramic views of the coastline, making every meal a memorable experience.

These establishments are just a glimpse of how the Amalfi Coast is catering to the evolving needs of modern travelers. Each place mentioned is accessible by foot or local transport, often found nestled in the heart of each town's vibrant streets or overlooking the scenic coast. The growing inclusivity in the region's culinary offerings ensures that everyone, regardless of dietary restrictions or preferences, can enjoy the rich flavors of the Amalfi Coast without compromise.

What I've loved most about exploring these options is not just the diversity of the food but also the willingness of local chefs and restaurateurs to embrace global food trends and dietary needs, all while maintaining the high standards and flavors Italy is known for. Whether you're a vegetarian looking for a hearty, plant-based meal, a vegan in search of dairy-free delights, or someone who needs gluten-free options, the Amalfi Coast's dining scene has evolved to welcome you with open arms and delicious dishes.

Culinary Courses and Food Tours

Exploring the Amalfi Coast through its culinary courses and food tours is like stepping into the soul of the region's culture. Every meal, every dish tells a story, and there's no better way to truly understand this than by rolling up your sleeves and immersing yourself in the art of Amalfi's cuisine. Over my travels, I've found that these experiences go beyond learning recipes—they're a chance to connect with local people, their traditions, and the very ingredients that make the food here so extraordinary.

One of my favorite experiences was taking a cooking class at Mamma Agata's Cooking School in Ravello. Nestled on a picturesque hillside at Piazza San Cosma, this school feels like visiting an old friend's home—if that friend happens to be an incredible chef. The class began with a walk through their garden, where I learned about the locally grown produce that would later be used in the dishes. The recipes were simple yet packed with flavor, focusing on regional classics like lemon chicken and handmade pasta. Classes here typically cost around $250 per person and include a multi-course meal that you prepare yourself, accompanied by wine pairings. Reservations are essential, and you can find more information at (https://www.mammaagata.com) or call +39 089 857019.

For a more hands-on adventure, I joined a food tour with Amalfi Lemon Experience, located at Via delle Cartiere, 55 in Amalfi. This unique experience dives deep into the region's famed lemons, from walking through lush lemon groves to learning how to make limoncello. The tour even included a cooking demonstration where we prepared dishes featuring the iconic citrus fruit. Prices for the tour range from $75 to $100 per person, and it's one of those experiences that left me with a newfound appreciation for Amalfi's lemons. They're easy to contact at +39 333 8446638 or via their website.

If you're in Positano, consider the Cooking Vacations Amalfi Coast experience. Located in the heart of the town, this program offers one-day classes or multi-day packages where you can master the art of making seafood risotto, tiramisu, and even pizzas from scratch. What made this stand out was the personal attention from the chefs and the setting—an open terrace overlooking Positano's iconic coastline. Classes start at $180 per person, and reservations can be made through their website.

These culinary adventures are more than just activities—they're an invitation into the kitchens and traditions of Amalfi Coast locals. What struck me most about these experiences was the emphasis on simplicity and quality. The cooking techniques are often straightforward, but the use of fresh, local ingredients transforms the simplest of recipes into something extraordinary. And the best part? You get to take these lessons home, carrying a little piece of the Amalfi Coast with you.

Participating in a food tour or culinary class is more than just a way to spend an afternoon—it's a way to see the Amalfi Coast from a different perspective, one that's rooted in its traditions and the warmth of its people. Whether you're kneading dough for fresh pasta or sipping homemade limoncello under the Mediterranean sun, these experiences will deepen your connection to this extraordinary region in ways that words—or even the most breathtaking views—simply cannot.

CHAPTER 5

Major Towns and Attractions

Positano: Colorful Villas and Chic Beachfront

Positano feels like it was made to be photographed. Its colorful villas cascade down the cliffs toward the turquoise sea, forming a picturesque vertical village that's as glamorous as it is inviting. Walking through the narrow, winding streets, I couldn't help but feel like I was stepping into a dream. The town's charm lies not just in its beauty but in its blend of laid-back coastal living and upscale sophistication. It's no wonder that Positano has been a magnet for travelers, artists, and writers for decades. The town's chic beachfront, Spiaggia Grande, is the hub of activity. Rows of bright orange and blue umbrellas line the beach, and you'll find everything from luxury loungers to casual spots for laying down a towel. This is where the glamour of Positano truly shines, with stylish visitors lounging by the water and others strolling along the promenade. The beach is also the starting point for boat tours, which I highly recommend—seeing Positano from the sea is a completely different perspective and one that's equally stunning.

While Positano's beauty is undeniable, the real magic happens when you start exploring its streets. The steep pathways are lined with boutiques selling handcrafted leather sandals, linen clothing, and ceramics that capture the vibrant colors of the town. One shop that caught my eye was Artigianato Rallo at Via dei Mulini, 16. It's the perfect place to pick up a unique souvenir, like a pair of custom-made sandals. For accommodations, Positano offers a range of options, each with its own personality and charm. Le Sirenuse, located at Via Cristoforo Colombo, 30, is one of the most iconic hotels in town. This luxury hotel offers stunning views of the bay, a Michelin-starred restaurant, and a gorgeous pool area. Rooms range from $500 to over $1,000 per night, depending on the season. You can contact them at +39 089 875066 or visit their website at (https://www.sirenuse.it).

If you're looking for something a bit more affordable but equally charming, Hotel Poseidon at Via Pasitea, 148, is a fantastic option. This family-run hotel combines traditional Positano charm with modern comforts, including a pool, a spa, and a terrace restaurant with panoramic views. Room rates typically range from $300 to $500 per night. They can be reached at +39 089 875067 or through their website at (https://www.hotelposeidonpositano.it). Dining in Positano is an experience in itself. For an unforgettable meal, La Sponda at Le Sirenuse is a must. The restaurant's candlelit ambiance and impeccable Mediterranean cuisine make it one of the most romantic spots in town. Expect to spend around $100 to $200 per person. Another favorite of mine is Da Vincenzo, located at Via Pasitea, 172/178. This cozy, family-run restaurant serves up authentic dishes like fresh seafood pasta and eggplant parmigiana. Prices here are more accessible, ranging from $30 to $70 per person. You can reach them at +39 089 875128 or visit their website at (https://www.davincenzo.it).

Getting to Positano is part of the adventure. If you're coming from Naples, you can take a train to Sorrento and then catch a SITA bus or a ferry directly to Positano. The ferry ride, in particular, is a treat, offering breathtaking views of the coastline as you approach the town. If you're driving, be prepared for narrow, winding roads and limited parking—many travelers choose to park in Sorrento and take public transport the rest of the way. Positano is a place that lives up to every bit of its reputation. It's vibrant, glamorous, and steeped in charm, with every corner offering something to discover.

Amalfi: Historical Sites and the Famous Cathedral

Amalfi, with its dramatic cliffs and deep blue waters, isn't just a visual marvel; it's steeped in history that dates back to the 6th century. Walking through this town, I always feel a sense of stepping back in time, especially when visiting the iconic Amalfi Cathedral (Duomo di Amalfi). Nestled in the heart of the town's main square, Piazza Duomo, the cathedral is a stunning example of medieval architecture that has stood as a beacon of Amalfi's cultural and spiritual life for centuries.

The Duomo's majestic staircase, a climb that's both literal and metaphorical into the town's rich history, leads to its striking façade adorned with a mix of Byzantine, Norman, and Gothic elements. Once inside, the cathedral's interior is just as impressive, with its ornate gold caisson ceiling and the serene Cloister of Paradise, known for its arched corridors that house ancient artifacts and beautifully frescoed walls. This cloister, adjacent to the cathedral, was originally built to provide a resting place for the town's illustrious citizens and now serves as a tranquil escape from the bustling square outside.

For those interested in the spiritual and architectural heritage of Amalfi, visiting the crypt where Saint Andrew's relics are kept is a must. It's not just a sacred visit but an encounter with the divine that has been revered by the faithful for generations. The relics, brought from Constantinople in 1206, underscore Amalfi's historical connections to the wider Mediterranean world.

After soaking up the history at the cathedral, I recommend exploring some of the local accommodations and eateries that make a stay in Amalfi truly memorable. Hotel Santa Caterina, located at Via Mauro Comite, 9, is an exemplary place to stay, providing luxury with cliffside views of the coastline. This hotel melds comfort with elegance, offering rooms and suites decorated in a classic style. Each stay here feels like a personal retreat, with prices ranging from $400 to $1,000 per night. For bookings, contact +39 089 871012 or visit (https://www.hotelsantacaterina.it).

For dining, Ristorante Marina Grande, on the beachfront at Viale della Regione, 4, is a standout choice. It offers a menu rich with local seafood prepared in traditional Amalfi style. The restaurant's setting allows diners to enjoy their meal accompanied by the sound of waves and a panoramic view of the Gulf. It's a culinary experience that's deeply rooted in the local culture, with prices ranging from $50 to $150 per person. Reservations can be made at +39 089 871129 or by visiting their website.

Getting to Amalfi is part of the adventure. The town is accessible via the winding SS163 coast road, known for its breathtaking views and thrilling turns. Alternatively, during the tourist season, ferries run frequently from Naples, Salerno, and Positano, offering a scenic route along the Tyrrhenian Sea to Amalfi's marina.

In Amalfi, history isn't just found in books or told in stories; it's lived and breathed. Each corner of this historic town offers a new narrative, each cobblestone path a passage through time. Whether you're here for the spectacular views, the deep historical roots, or the warm local hospitality, Amalfi promises an experience that's as enriching as it is enchanting.

Atrani: Charming Seaside Village with Picturesque Views

Nestled just a stone's throw from the more bustling Amalfi, Atrani offers a slice of coastal charm that is often overlooked by the typical tourist trail. This quaint village, with its tightly woven alleyways and picturesque square, allows you to experience the authentic life of the Amalfi Coast without the crowds. My journey through Atrani was marked by serene walks, delightful discoveries around each corner, and the unmistakable aroma of Italian cuisine wafting through the air.

Atrani's appeal lies in its simplicity and small-scale beauty. The village is centered around Piazza Umberto I, a cozy square that feels like the living room of the community. Here, locals gather to chat, children play freely, and visitors are welcomed with open arms and warm smiles. The square is lined with a few cafes and restaurants that serve as the perfect backdrop for soaking in the atmosphere and enjoying some local fare. For those looking to stay overnight, Palazzo Ferraioli is a delightful choice. Located on Via Campo, 16, this boutique hotel is housed in a renovated historic building and offers stunning views of both the sea and the surrounding cliffs. The hotel combines modern amenities with traditional décor, creating a luxurious yet comfortable setting. Each room is uniquely decorated, reflecting the maritime heritage of the area. Rates typically range from $150 to $300 per night, offering value for the exceptional quality and location. You can contact them at +39 089 871588 or visit their website. (https://www.palazzoferraioli.it) for more details.

Dining in Atrani is a treat, with several hidden gems that boast some of the best traditional Italian dishes on the coast. Le Palme restaurant, situated right in Piazza Umberto I, is a favorite among both locals and visitors. Known for its fresh seafood and pasta, the restaurant also offers a charming terrace that overlooks the square. Meals here are reasonably priced, with dinner options ranging from $20 to $50 per person, making it accessible for a variety of budgets. For reservations, call +39 089 871324 or drop by—they're welcoming to walk-ins, which reflects the village's laid-back vibe. Accessing Atrani is a breeze, particularly due to its proximity to Amalfi. A scenic walk from Amalfi along the coastal road takes about ten minutes and is as picturesque as it is refreshing. Alternatively, SITA buses frequently run between Amalfi and Atrani, making the village easily reachable for those coming from further afield. In Atrani, the pace of life slows, and the beauty of the Amalfi Coast shines through in its most undisturbed form. This village, though small, offers a rich experience characterized by its scenic beauty, historical architecture, and the warm hospitality of its residents. It's a place where you can wander without a map, discover local artisans, and indulge in the culinary delights of authentic Italian cuisine.

Ravello: Gardens, Villas, and Music Festivals

Nestled high above the Amalfi Coast, Ravello is a serene escape known for its breathtaking views, lush gardens, and rich cultural life. This charming town has long been a haven for artists, writers, and musicians, drawn by its quiet beauty and inspiring atmosphere. My visits to Ravello have always felt like stepping into a living painting, where the vibrant greens of the gardens contrast with the deep blue of the Mediterranean sky.

One of the jewels of Ravello is the Villa Rufolo, located at Piazza Duomo, Ravello. This historic villa, with origins dating back to the 13th century, is famous not only for its stunning architecture but also for its beautiful cascading gardens. Walking through these gardens, you're treated to panoramic views that overlook the coastline—a sight so striking that it famously inspired Richard Wagner in the composition of his opera, Parsifal. The gardens are a favorite spot for visitors, especially during the summer months when they become the stage for the Ravello Festival, an annual celebration of music and arts that fills the town with melodies and performances from around the world. Contact information for Villa Rufolo is available at +39 089 857621 or through their website, where you can also find event schedules and ticket prices.

Accommodations in Ravello cater to a range of preferences, from luxurious hotels to charming bed and breakfasts. One of the most renowned places to stay is the Belmond Hotel Caruso, located at Piazza San Giovanni del Toro 2. This former 11th-century palace offers rooms with elegant decor and terraced gardens that seem to float between sea and sky. The hotel features a stunning infinity pool, from which you can see across the mountains and waters of the Amalfi Coast. Room rates start around $500 per night, reaching up to $2000 during peak season. For more details, visit their website or call +39 089 858801.

For dining in Ravello, Rossellinis at the Belmond Hotel Caruso offers a fine dining experience with a Michelin-starred menu that highlights local ingredients in a sophisticated setting. A meal here is a delightful journey through the flavors of Campania, complemented by the restaurant's extensive wine list and the unforgettable views from its terraces. Dining costs range from $100 to $200 per person, and reservations can be made at +39 089 858801 or through the hotel's website.

If you're looking for something a bit more casual but equally memorable, Cumpa' Cosimo, located on Via Roma, 44, offers a taste of traditional Italian cuisine in a warm, family-run setting. Known for its hearty portions and friendly service, this restaurant is a favorite among locals and tourists alike. Prices are more moderate here, with meals typically ranging from $25 to $50 per person. You can reach them at +39 089 857156.

Getting to Ravello involves a winding journey up the mountain roads that can be quite an adventure in itself. The town is accessible by SITA bus from Amalfi, which offers a scenic route up the hillside. Alternatively, you can drive or take a taxi from Amalfi, which gives you the flexibility to explore at your own pace.

Ravello is more than just a destination; it's an experience. The combination of its artistic heritage, architectural wonders, and the natural beauty of its gardens and views creates a unique atmosphere that captivates everyone who visits. Whether you're coming for the tranquility, the culture, or simply to escape the more crowded spots along the coast, Ravello offers a peaceful yet enriching retreat into the heart of the Italian landscape.

Sorrento: Vibrant Nightlife and Gateway to Capri

Sorrento, perched on the cliffs of the Sorrentine Peninsula, serves as a vibrant gateway to the Amalfi Coast and the island of Capri. This bustling town is not only a strategic base for exploring the region but also a lively destination in its own right, especially noted for its dynamic nightlife and charming old-world atmosphere.

The lively energy of Sorrento is palpable as soon as the sun sets. The town's narrow, cobbled streets come alive with locals and tourists alike, drawn by the allure of its bustling bars, elegant lounges, and lively music venues. Piazza Tasso, Sorrento's central square, transforms into a vibrant hub of activity where outdoor cafes spill over with patrons enjoying the cool evening air. Here, the conversation flows as freely as the local limoncello, and you can feel the genuine warmth of Sorrentine hospitality.

One of the hottest spots for experiencing Sorrento's nightlife is Fauno Bar, located right in the heart of Piazza Tasso. This popular bar is perfect for people-watching and soaking in the local scene. With a wide selection of drinks and often live music or DJ sets, it's a prime location to while away an evening. A night out here can vary in cost, but you can expect to spend around $20 to $40 per person for a few drinks and snacks. For more details or to make a reservation, you can contact them at +39 081 878 1135 or visit their website.

For accommodations, Sorrento offers a range of options, from luxurious hotels to charming B&Bs. Grand Hotel Excelsior Vittoria, located at Piazza Tasso, 34, is one of the most prestigious addresses in town. Set in a unique location with spectacular views over the Bay of Naples, this historic hotel combines luxury with tradition and has lush, terraced gardens that add to its tranquil feel. Room rates typically start at around $400 per night and can go up to $1000 during peak season. You can book a room by calling +39 081 877 7111 or visiting their website (https://www.exvitt.it).

For a dining experience that matches the elegance of Sorrento itself, Ristorante Bagni Delfino, located at Via Marina Grande, 216, is a must-visit. Nestled on the waterfront, this restaurant offers stunning views of the sea alongside a menu filled with fresh seafood, perfectly cooked pasta, and a variety of local specialties. Dining here is not just a meal; it's an experience, with main courses typically ranging from $30 to $50. Reservations are recommended, especially in the summer months, and can be made at +39 081 878 2038 or through their website (https://www.bagnidelfino.com).

Getting to Sorrento is quite straightforward, with the town being well-connected by train, bus, and ferry. The Circumvesuviana train from Naples offers a scenic route into the heart of Sorrento, and the journey itself is an adventure, winding through small towns and lush countryside before arriving at Sorrento's bustling station.

In Sorrento, the blend of lively street life, stunning natural scenery, and rich cultural experiences makes for a memorable stay. Whether you're sipping a cocktail at a bustling piazza, dining by the moonlit sea, or exploring the town's historical sites, Sorrento offers a perfect mix of relaxation and excitement, making it an ideal stop on any journey along the Amalfi Coast.

Nerano: Secluded Beaches and Culinary Excellence

Nerano, a charming hamlet nestled at the southern tip of the Sorrento Peninsula, is a gem within the Amalfi Coast that offers tranquility away from the hustle and bustle of the more frequented tourist spots. This secluded village is renowned for its spectacular beaches and its culinary prowess, particularly its seafood and pasta dishes that are as authentic as they are delicious. My visits to Nerano have always been highlighted by lazy days spent on its pebbled shores and evenings indulging in some of the best food the region has to offer.

The main allure of Nerano is its stunning coastline, which includes the famous Marina del Cantone. This beach is a haven for those seeking a quieter seaside experience, with crystal-clear waters perfect for swimming and snorkeling. The beach is lined with several small, family-run establishments where you can rent sun loungers and umbrellas for a day under the Italian sun. Access to Marina del Cantone is straightforward, with a road leading directly to the beach from the center of Nerano, easily accessible by car or local bus services from Sorrento.

Accommodation options in Nerano are reflective of its serene environment. Casale Villarena, located in Via Amerigo Vespucci, offers guests a more intimate experience. This historic residence features comfortable apartments with stunning views of the Mediterranean and includes access to a private pool, an on-site restaurant, and beautiful gardens. The hospitality here is unmatched, making you feel like part of the family. Rates range from $150 to $300 per night, varying by season and room type. For more information or to make a reservation, contact them at +39 081 808 1779 or visit their website at (https://www.casalevillarena.com).

Dining in Nerano is an event in itself, especially with restaurants like Ristorante Maria Grazia. This eatery, located directly on the Marina del Cantone, is famous for inventing "Spaghetti alla Nerano," a simple yet delicious dish made with zucchini, parmesan, and basil. The restaurant's setting allows diners to enjoy their meals with the sound of waves lapping against the shore—a truly idyllic experience. Expect to spend around $35 to $70 per person, depending on your choice of dishes and drinks. Reservations can be made at +39 081 808 1011 or through their website.

Getting to Nerano is easiest by car, allowing the flexibility to explore the winding roads at your own pace. Alternatively, SITA buses run regularly from Sorrento, providing a scenic and cost-effective way to reach this picturesque village. The journey itself is part of the charm, offering breathtaking views as you descend towards the coast.

In Nerano, life moves slowly, and the emphasis is on enjoying every moment, whether it's a day spent sunbathing on its pristine beaches or an evening savoring the culinary delights that make this village a food lover's paradise. Each visit here reaffirms my love for the simpler things in life—stunning scenery, good food, and warm hospitality. It's a place that encourages you to pause, breathe, and indulge in the pleasures of coastal Italian living.

Cetara: Authentic Fishing Village with Famous Anchovies

Tucked away on the Amalfi Coast, the village of Cetara offers a glimpse into the authentic life of a traditional Italian fishing community. Known for its deep connection to the sea, particularly for its anchovies and "colatura di alici" (anchovy sauce), Cetara captures the essence of coastal living with its bustling harbor, vibrant local life, and culinary excellence.

As I wandered through the narrow streets of Cetara, the salty air mixed with the aromas of freshly cooked seafood was instantly welcoming. The village is compact, with everything within walking distance, which perfectly adds to its charm. The main beach, though small, is picturesque and provides a lovely spot for a swim with views of the surrounding cliffs.

Accommodations in Cetara are charming and mostly family-run, offering a warm, personal touch. Hotel Cetus, located at Via Lauro 6, is one of the standout places to stay. Perched above the sea, it offers rooms with stunning views and first-class amenities, including a fine dining restaurant that specializes in seafood. The prices typically range from $150 to $300 per night, depending on the season. For bookings, you can reach them at +39 089 261039 or check out their website at (https://www.hotelcetus.com).

Dining in Cetara is a treat for anyone who loves seafood. Ristorante San Pietro stands out as a local favorite. Located at Via Marina, 2, this restaurant offers a menu that is a tribute to the sea, with dishes like spaghetti with anchovies and the famous "acqua pazza" fish cooked in a watery, herbed broth. The ambiance is casual yet inviting, and meals are reasonably priced from $25 to $50 per person. You can call them at +39 089 261091 or visit their website for more details.

Getting to Cetara is straightforward. The village is well-connected by road and is just a short drive from Salerno, making it accessible by car, bus, or even by ferry during the summer months. The journey along the coastal road offers spectacular views, making the drive part of the Cetara experience.

In Cetara, the pace of life slows down, allowing visitors to soak in the simple pleasures of village life. Whether it's watching the fishermen bring in their daily catch, enjoying a meal of fresh anchovies, or just strolling along the marina, Cetara offers a unique taste of the Amalfi Coast that is both grounding and utterly enchanting. Every visit here reminds me why I cherish these small, less-touristed towns—they offer a genuine connection to local traditions and a chance to appreciate the natural beauty and culinary richness of Italy.

Maiori: Expansive Beaches and Historic Churches

Maiori is a treasure along the Amalfi Coast, known for its expansive sandy beach which is quite a rarity in a region characterized by rugged cliffs and petite coves. This makes Maiori especially appealing for families and those looking for a more relaxed beach experience. The town also boasts a rich history, evidenced by its ancient churches and charming architecture. Each time I visit Maiori, I am taken by its understated beauty and the laid-back atmosphere that is a stark contrast to some of its more bustling neighbors.

Maiori's beach, with its broad, welcoming stretch of sand and lapping waves, is perfect for sunbathing, building sandcastles, or simply taking a gentle stroll along the water's edge. The promenade backing the beach is lined with a variety of cafes and gelaterias, providing ample opportunity to grab a refreshing drink or a tasty treat while enjoying views of the Mediterranean.

For those interested in exploring the historical aspect of Maiori, the Church of Santa Maria a Mare is a must-visit. This church, perched atop a hill, offers not only spiritual solace but also stunning views over the town and the coastline. Its majolica-tiled dome and rich history dating back to the 12th century make it a focal point for anyone fascinated by the region's deep cultural roots.

When it comes to accommodations, Hotel Panorama at Via Santa Tecla, 8, stands out due to its prime location right on the waterfront and its top-notch facilities which include a rooftop pool, a private beach area, and rooms with sea views. The rates here vary from about $150 to $300 per night depending on the season. You can get in touch with them at +39 089 877 177 or check their availability at (https://www.hotelpanorama.it).

Dining in Maiori offers a slice of Italian culinary excellence, with Ristorante Masaniello being a particular favorite. Situated conveniently along Corso Regina, 10, Masaniello specializes in seafood that's freshly caught and exquisitely prepared. The ambiance is warm and welcoming, with a decor that reflects the maritime heritage of the town. A meal here can cost between $30 and $60 per person, a fair price for some of the best local cuisine. For reservations, contact +39 089 877183 or visit their website.

Getting to Maiori is quite straightforward whether you are driving or using public transport. The town is well-connected by the SITA Sud bus service that runs along the Amalfi Coast, making stops in all major towns including Amalfi, from where Maiori is just a short ride away. If driving, the scenic Strada Statale 163 offers a breathtaking approach to Maiori, though be prepared for narrow winding roads typical of the region.

In Maiori, the blend of expansive beaches, historic sites, and exceptional dining creates a perfect setting for anyone looking to immerse themselves in the tranquil yet enriching lifestyle of the Amalfi Coast. Whether you're lounging on the beach, exploring ancient churches, or savoring the local cuisine, Maiori provides a backdrop that combines relaxation with cultural enrichment, making every visit memorable.

Furore: The Famous Fjord and Unique Hiking Trails

Furore, often referred to as "the town that doesn't exist" because of its hidden location, is one of the Amalfi Coast's most unique treasures. Nestled between cliffs, the village is famous not just for its discreet charm but for the stunning Furore Fjord, a narrow gorge that reaches the sea. My first visit to Furore was like uncovering a secret sanctuary, where the dramatic landscapes and the tranquil atmosphere create a sense of wonder that's hard to find elsewhere.

The Fjord of Furore, with its pebbly beach and old fishermen's houses painted in bright colors, is a breathtaking sight. The small beach at the fjord's base is accessible via a staircase that winds down the gorge, offering picturesque views at every turn. This hidden cove, where the sea gently laps against the shore, provides a serene escape from the more crowded spots along the coast. For hiking enthusiasts, Furore offers some of the most scenic trails in the region. The Path of the Gods, a famous hiking trail, starts from Agerola, a nearby hilltop town, and ends in Positano. Along the way, it offers incredible vistas of the Amalfi Coast, and walking this path has been one of the most memorable experiences of my travels, filled with panoramic views that are simply unforgettable.

Accommodations in Furore cater to those looking for peace and intimacy. La Locanda del Fiordo, located at Via Trasita 9, is a boutique hotel perched right above the fjord. With terraces that offer expansive views of the sea and a hot tub to relax in after a day of hiking, it's a perfect retreat. Room rates typically range from $100 to $250 per night, offering good value for the experience. For more details or to make a booking, you can contact them at +39 089 830 015 or visit their website at (http://www.locandadelfiordo.com).

Dining in Furore is a delightful experience, with several restaurants serving fresh seafood and local dishes. Hostaria di Bacco, located at Via G. B. Lama 9, stands out for its culinary excellence. The restaurant offers a terrace with stunning views of the coast and specializes in traditional dishes made with local ingredients, such as homemade pasta and freshly caught fish. Dining here is not just eating; it's an experience, with meal prices ranging from $35 to $60 per person. To reserve a table, you can call +39 089 830 360 or check out their offerings on their website.

Getting to Furore involves a bit of adventure. The village is situated halfway between Amalfi and Positano and can be reached by the SITA Sud bus connecting these towns. The stop "Furore" drops you on the main road, from where you can walk down to the fjord or to your accommodation. If driving, be prepared for narrow winding roads that are typical for the Amalfi Coast but offer dramatic and beautiful scenery. Furore's blend of natural beauty, tranquility, and rustic charm makes it an exceptional destination on the Amalfi Coast.

Vietri sul Mare: Renowned Ceramics and Coastal Charm

Vietri sul Mare, often considered the gateway to the Amalfi Coast, is a town where Italian ceramic artistry shines brightly, surrounded by the magnetic charm of a coastal village steeped in history. As I strolled through Vietri's vibrant streets on my first visit, I was instantly struck by the kaleidoscope of colors from the beautifully adorned pottery displayed in every shop window. Each piece, from intricately painted plates to elegant vases, tells a story of traditional craftsmanship passed down through generations.

Vietri sul Mare's reputation as the center of ceramics in the Amalfi Coast is not just a title; it's an identity that permeates every aspect of the town. The Ceramiche d'Arte Carmela located at Via Cristoforo Colombo, 32, is a must-visit. This studio and shop is where you can witness first-hand the meticulous skill of local artisans and perhaps even try your hand at pottery-making in one of their workshops. The vivid designs reflect the sea, the sky, and the landscapes of the Amalfi Coast, making these ceramics true works of art and fantastic souvenirs.

When it comes to accommodations, Vietri offers a range of options that highlight the town's cozy charm and artistic flair. Hotel Raito, situated at Via Nuova Raito, 9, is a particularly stunning place to stay. This five-star hotel boasts panoramic views of the coastline, with rooms that blend modern luxury with touches of local style. The hotel also features two swimming pools, a spa, and a fine dining restaurant specializing in regional cuisine. Room rates typically start around $200 per night, and can go up to $400 during peak season. For more information or to make a booking, you can call them at +39 089 763 4111 or visit their website at (https://www.hotelraito.it).

Dining in Vietri sul Mare is a joy, particularly at Ristorante Il Principe e La Civetta, located at Via

Osvaldo Costabile 31. This restaurant offers a delightful taste of local seafood and traditional Italian dishes, served in a charming setting with views of the sea. The ambiance is warm and welcoming, making it a perfect spot for both romantic dinners and family meals. The cost of a meal ranges from $30 to $60 per person. Reservations can be made at +39 089 763 003 or through their website (http://www.ilprincipeelacivetta.com).

Getting to Vietri sul Mare is straightforward, whether you're coming by car, train, or bus. The town is just off the A3 motorway, making it easily accessible by car. Additionally, Vietri is serviced by regional trains from Naples and Salerno, with the train station located just a short walk from the town center. In Vietri sul Mare, the blend of artistic heritage and Mediterranean charm creates a unique cultural experience.

Praiano: Serene Getaway and Stunning Sunsets

Praiano, a serene village perched between the bustling towns of Positano and Amalfi, offers a tranquil retreat on the Amalfi Coast. Known for its breathtaking sunsets and quieter atmosphere, Praiano is a haven for those looking to escape the more tourist-heavy locales. The first time I visited, I was captivated by the stunning panoramas at every turn and the soothing sound of the waves crashing against the rugged coastline.

Praiano's charm is most apparent during the golden hours of dusk, when the sky turns a palette of fiery colors and the sea glows with reflections of the setting sun. The town's vantage points, especially around the Church of San Gennaro with its beautiful ceramic-tiled plaza, offer some of the best views for sunset watching. It's a moment that connects you deeply with the serene beauty of this coastal haven.

For accommodations, Hotel Tramonto d'Oro, located at Via Gennaro Capriglione 119, stands out for its exceptional service and stunning sea views. This family-run hotel embodies the warmth of Italian hospitality and features a rooftop terrace that is perfect for enjoying the famed sunsets of Praiano. The hotel also boasts a swimming pool and a restaurant that serves local specialties. Room rates vary from about $200 to $500 per night, making it an excellent value for the luxury and comfort provided. For more information or to make a reservation, you can contact them at +39 089 874955 or visit their website at (https://www.tramontodoro.com).

Dining in Praiano offers a delightful experience at Ristorante Il Pirata, located at Via Terramare. Nestled by the water's edge, this restaurant provides a romantic setting where you can dine on fresh seafood while listening to the sound of the waves. The restaurant is famed for its creative dishes that highlight the freshness of the Amalfi

Coast's bounty. Expect to spend around $40 to $80 per person for a meal that is both memorable and satisfying. For booking, call +39 089 874377 or check their details online.

Getting to Praiano is relatively straightforward, though it involves some navigation through winding coastal roads. The SITA Sud bus service connects Praiano with both Positano to the west and Amalfi to the east, making it accessible via public transportation. Additionally, renting a scooter can be an exhilarating way to explore Praiano and its surroundings at your own pace, allowing you to discover secluded spots along the coast. In Praiano, life slows down, and the emphasis is on enjoying the natural beauty and peaceful environment. Whether you're lounging on one of its small beaches, exploring local art galleries, or simply sipping a glass of Limoncello while watching the sunset, Praiano provides a perfect blend of relaxation and understated elegance.

Salerno and Via dei Mercanti: Vibrant Port City with Iconic Shopping Streets

Salerno, often overlooked in favor of its more famous Amalfi Coast neighbors, is a vibrant port city that boasts a rich history, dynamic culture, and bustling modern life. My first visit to Salerno revealed a city that perfectly blends its medieval past with contemporary charm, especially notable along the iconic Via dei Mercanti, a bustling shopping street that runs through the heart of its historic center.

Walking through Via dei Mercanti is like traversing through time. The street is lined with a mix of traditional boutiques, modern shops, and lively cafes, where locals and visitors alike mingle. The architecture here tells the story of Salerno's layered history, from Roman times through to the Middle Ages and into the modern era. This street is not just a place for shopping; it's a hub of daily life, reflecting the vibrant community spirit of Salerno.

Accommodation options in Salerno cater to all tastes and budgets, but Hotel Plaza at Piazza Vittorio Veneto, 42 stands out for its central location and excellent service. Just steps from the main train station and a short walk to the waterfront, this hotel offers clean, comfortable rooms with views of the city buzz. Rates typically range from $100 to $150 per night, providing great value given its proximity to key attractions and transport links. For more details or to book a room, you can contact them at +39 089 224477 or visit their website at (https://www.hotelplazasalerno.it).

Dining in Salerno is a delightful experience, especially at Ristorante Cicirinella, located at Via dei Mercanti, 68. This restaurant serves traditional Southern Italian cuisine with a focus on fresh, local ingredients. Known for its seafood dishes and homemade pasta, Cicirinella offers a warm, inviting atmosphere that pairs perfectly with their exquisite food. A meal here typically costs between $30 and $50 per person, which is reasonable for the high quality of food and service. To make a reservation, call +39 089 296 2025.

Getting to Salerno is straightforward, thanks to its excellent transport connections. The city has a major train station with high-speed rail links to Rome and Naples, making it an accessible gateway for exploring the Amalfi Coast and beyond. Additionally, the local buses and ferries provide easy access to nearby coastal towns and attractions, making Salerno an ideal base for regional exploration.

Salerno's blend of historical depth, cultural vibrancy, and modern amenities makes it a compelling destination for anyone looking to experience a different side of the Amalfi Coast.

CHAPTER 6

Northern Amalfi Coast

Sorrento: Rich History and Access to Capri

Sorrento, nestled on the cliffs of the Northern Amalfi Coast, is a city where every corner has a story to tell. Known for its rich history and as a gateway to the enchanting island of Capri, Sorrento captivates with its blend of tradition, beauty, and cultural depth. The charm of this town is in its old-world feel, combined with the panoramic vistas of the Bay of Naples and Mount Vesuvius in the distance. On my first visit, the vibrancy of Sorrento's streets, filled with the scent of lemon groves and the sound of the sea, left a lasting impression.

Exploring Sorrento offers a journey through time, from the ancient ruins of the Roman times to the grand churches of the medieval era and the elegant boutiques and cafes that line the streets today. Piazza Tasso, the main square, is the heart of the city, bustling with life and framed by historic buildings.

For those looking to stay in Sorrento, Grand Hotel Excelsior Vittoria at Piazza Tasso 34 offers a luxurious experience with stunning views over the harbor. This historic hotel, dating back to the 1800s, combines elegance with modern amenities, providing a perfect base to explore the area. Prices typically range from $300 to $600 per night, reflecting its premium offerings and exceptional location. Contact them at +39 081 877 7111 or visit their website at (htttps://www.exvitt.it) for more details.

Dining in Sorrento is a treat, with Ristorante Bagni Delfino at Via Marina Grande 216 standing out for its exquisite seafood and waterfront dining. Sitting on the pier, this restaurant offers a mesmerizing view of the sea, making it an ideal spot for a romantic dinner. Expect to spend around $50 to $100 per person for a meal that features the freshest local ingredients. Reservations can be made at +39 081 878 2038 or through their website.

Getting to Sorrento is straightforward, with the town being well connected by road, rail, and sea. The Circumvesuviana rail line from Naples provides an easy and scenic route to Sorrento, making it accessible for day-trippers and long-stay tourists alike. Additionally, ferries from Naples dock directly at Sorrento's marina, offering another picturesque way to arrive. Sorrento's accessibility to Capri is one of its most compelling features. Ferries regularly make the short journey across the water, providing stunning views along the way and connecting visitors to the famed beauty of Capri within minutes. In Sorrento, the rich history seamlessly integrates with the dynamic present.

Massa Lubrense: Natural Beauty and Quiet Villages

Massa Lubrense, a captivating gem on the Northern Amalfi Coast, offers a tranquil escape into a world where nature's beauty and quiet village life are wonderfully preserved. As I meandered through the lush landscapes and quaint hamlets of Massa Lubrense on my first visit, I felt as though I had stepped into a slower-paced, more contemplative world, away from the bustling tourist spots further along the coast.

This area is renowned for its spectacular views, especially from points like Punta Campanella, where the vistas stretch across the sea to the island of Capri. The terrain here is a hiker's paradise, with trails winding through olive groves and citrus orchards, leading to secluded coves that many visitors to the Amalfi Coast miss.

For those seeking accommodation, Hotel Delfino at Via Nastro d'Oro, 2, stands out with its breathtaking sea views and excellent customer service. Nestled on a cliff overlooking the water, this hotel offers a peaceful retreat with a private beach access, a saltwater swimming pool, and a restaurant serving local specialties. The rates here are quite reasonable for the Amalfi Coast, ranging from $150 to $300 per night. For bookings, contact them at +39 081 878 9261 or visit their website at (https://www.hoteldelfino.com).

Dining in Massa Lubrense is a delightful experience, with restaurants like Ristorante Le Sirene at Via delle Sirene, 15, offering a menu that celebrates the best of local produce and freshly caught seafood. Dining here, you're likely to find dishes infused with the region's famous lemons and herbs, enjoyed on a terrace with views that make every meal memorable. Expect to spend around $40 to $70 per person, a worthy investment for the quality of food and the idyllic setting. Reservations can be made at +39 081 808 1056.

Getting to Massa Lubrense involves a scenic drive along the coastal road from Sorrento. The journey itself is part of the experience, with stunning vistas around every turn. Public transport options include regular buses from Sorrento, which make stops in various parts of Massa Lubrense, allowing for easy access to different areas within the commune.

In Massa Lubrense, the connection to nature is palpable. Whether you're exploring the protected marine area of Punta Campanella or enjoying a quiet moment in a village piazza, the area offers a sense of peace and authenticity that is both refreshing and profound. Each visit here deepens my appreciation for the quieter, less trodden paths of the Amalfi Coast, where the beauty of the landscape and the simplicity of village life provide a perfect backdrop for relaxation and reflection.

CHAPTER 7

Southern Amalfi Coast

Amalfi: Historical Gems and Cultural Highlights

Exploring Amalfi on the southern coast, I quickly discovered why this town is more than just a name on a map—it's a tapestry woven with vibrant historical and cultural threads. Nestled at the mouth of a deep ravine and towering cliffs, Amalfi boasts a maritime history that once positioned it as a maritime superpower. Today, it's the stunning architecture and the remnants of its illustrious past that capture the imagination.

The centerpiece of Amalfi's rich historical tapestry is undoubtedly the Cathedral of Saint Andrew, with its striking façade and majestic staircase that dominates the town's main square. Venturing inside, the blend of architectural styles tells the story of Amalfi's evolution through the ages, and the crypt houses the relics of Saint Andrew, adding a profound spiritual dimension to this historical site.

Accommodation options in Amalfi cater to a variety of tastes and budgets. One standout is the Hotel Luna Convento at Via Pantaleone Comite 33. This hotel's history as a 12th-century convent contributes to its unique charm, coupled with breathtaking views of the coast. The serene cloisters and an Arab-Norman architecture provide a peaceful retreat. Room rates here range from $250 to $500 per night, offering a luxurious stay that reflects the historical essence of Amalfi. For reservations, their contact number is +39 089 871002, and more information can be found on their website at (https://www.hotellunaamalfi.com). For dining, Ristorante Marina Grande on Viale della Regione, 4 stands out with its beachfront setting and a menu that highlights the best of local seafood. The experience of dining here, with the sound of waves and a view under the stars, is simply magical. The dishes, infused with locally sourced ingredients, encapsulate the culinary heritage of the region. A meal here ranges from $35 to $70 per person, blending quality with a memorable atmosphere. Book a table at +39 089 871129 or visit (http://www.ristorantemarinagrande.com).

Reaching Amalfi is part of the adventure, accessible via the serpentine Amalfi Drive (SS163) known for its stunning vistas. Whether arriving by bus from Sorrento or by ferry from Positano, the journey into Amalfi is as breathtaking as the destination itself. In Amalfi, every cobblestone and corner offers a gateway to the past, from the bustling piazzas to the quiet backstreets that reveal intricate details of medieval stonework. The cultural vibrancy of the town is palpable, not just in its architecture and historical sites but also in the warmth of its people who are the custodians of this magnificent heritage.

Praiano: Serene Getaway and Path of the Gods

Praiano, a serene and picturesque village nestled on the Southern Amalfi Coast, offers a captivating blend of natural beauty and tranquility that stands out even in a region celebrated for its stunning landscapes. Unlike its more bustling neighbors, Praiano provides a quiet retreat, perfect for those seeking peace amidst the Mediterranean's scenic splendor.

One of Praiano's crowning jewels is the Path of the Gods, a hiking trail that offers some of the most breathtaking views over the coast. Walking this path, it's easy to understand how it got its name; the vistas are simply divine, stretching out over the sparkling Tyrrhenian Sea with views of Capri and Positano in the distance. Starting from Praiano, the trail weaves through terraced vineyards and ancient stone houses, enveloped by the aromatic wild herbs of the Mediterranean maquis.

For those planning to stay, Hotel Margherita at Via Umberto I, 70, is an excellent choice. This family-run hotel provides a warm welcome that epitomizes Italian hospitality. With a panoramic terrace overlooking the sea and a swimming pool surrounded by lemon trees, it's a peaceful haven to return to after a day of exploration. Room rates range from $150 to $250 per night, depending on the season. For more information or to make a reservation, you can contact them at +39 089 874628 or visit their website at (https://www.hotelmargherita.info).

When it comes to dining in Praiano, Ristorante Il Pirata located at Via Terramare, offers a culinary experience as memorable as the views. Situated right by the water's edge, this restaurant specializes in seafood, with dishes that are a testament to the freshness and quality of local catch. Dining here, especially at sunset, is an experience that combines the best of Amalfi Coast flavors with the enchanting ambiance of the sea. Meals typically cost between $30 to $60 per person. You can book a table by calling +39 089 874377 or visiting their online portal.

Reaching Praiano is straightforward yet scenic. Whether you're driving along the winding coastal roads from Amalfi or taking a local SITA Sud bus from Positano, the journey is part of the Praiano experience, filled with picturesque views at every turn.

Praiano is not just a destination; it's a retreat for the soul. Here, the pace slows, the mind rests, and the beauty of the Amalfi Coast can be appreciated in its most authentic form. Whether lounging on its small pebble beaches, exploring hidden coves, or just sitting back at a café watching the world go by, Praiano offers a slice of coastal paradise that remains etched in the heart long after the visit.

CHAPTER 8

Eastern Amalfi Coast

Minori and Maiori: Traditional Coastal Life and Lemon Groves

As I ventured into Minori and Maiori on the Eastern Amalfi Coast, I was immediately struck by their serene beauty and the lush lemon groves that define much of the landscape here. These twin towns, though less famous than some of their western neighbors, offer a glimpse into the traditional coastal life that has sustained this region for centuries.

Minori, with its intimate beachfront and historic sites, is particularly known for its ancient Roman villa, which beautifully illustrates the town's long history. Wandering through its well-preserved ruins, I could almost hear the echoes of the past, blending seamlessly with the gentle waves lapping against the shore. Maiori, on the other hand, boasts the longest beach of the Amalfi Coast, lined with a lively promenade that invites leisurely strolls and offers ample spots to just sit and soak up the Mediterranean sun.

For accommodations, Hotel Santa Lucia in Minori at Via Nazionale 44 offers a welcoming atmosphere with superb service, nestled right in the heart of the town. Its proximity to both the beach and historical sites makes it an ideal spot for those looking to explore the area thoroughly. Rooms here are comfortably priced between $100 and $200 per night, and you can contact them at +39 089 877191 or check their offerings at (https://www.hotelsantalucia.it).

Dining in these towns is a delight, especially at Ristorante Giardiniello in Minori at Via Vittorio Emanuele 17. This charming restaurant offers a true taste of the Amalfi Coast with dishes that highlight fresh local ingredients, including seafood caught daily and, of course, the famous lemons grown right in their backyard. Expect to spend about $30 to $50 per person for a meal that's sure to be memorable. Reservations can be made at +39 089 877050, or you can visit their website for more details.

Getting to Minori and Maiori is part of the adventure, with several options available. The towns are accessible by the SITA Sud bus from Salerno, which provides a scenic route along the coast. For those driving, the coastal road offers stunning views and the freedom to explore at your own pace.

In Minori and Maiori, the connection between the land, the sea, and the people is palpable. From the vibrant flavors of the local cuisine to the sweet fragrance of lemon groves and the salt air, every element here is a testament to the enduring allure of coastal living.

Salerno: Medieval History and Modern Vibe

As I explored Salerno on the Eastern Amalfi Coast, I was immediately captivated by its unique blend of medieval history and modern vibrancy. This dynamic city, with its deep historical roots and contemporary pulse, offers an intriguing contrast to the traditional Amalfi Coast towns with their quaint charm.

Salerno's heart is its historic center, where ancient walls and narrow lanes tell tales of a past that dates back to the Roman and Byzantine eras. The crowning jewel here is the Salerno Cathedral, a stunning example of medieval architecture that houses the relics of St. Matthew. Venturing inside, the cathedral's crypt and ornate frescoes provide a profound sense of the city's rich religious and cultural heritage. For accommodations, Grand Hotel Salerno at Lungomare Clemente Tafuri, 1 is a standout. Perfectly located near the waterfront, this hotel offers easy access to the city's main attractions and the vibrant nightlife that Salerno is known for. With room rates ranging from $120 to $250 per night, it provides a mix of comfort and luxury that caters to both leisure and business travelers. You can reach them at +39 089 7041111 or check their website at (https://www.grandhotelsalerno.com) for more information.

Dining in Salerno is a delight at Ristorante Cicirinella at Via Trotula De Ruggiero, 7. Here, traditional Southern Italian cuisine meets innovation in dishes that highlight local ingredients like buffalo mozzarella and San Marzano tomatoes. The restaurant's cozy atmosphere and friendly service make it a local favorite, with meals priced around $25 to $50 per person. For reservations, call +39 089 226129 or visit their website to explore their menu.

Getting to Salerno is straightforward, with excellent train connections from major Italian cities to Salerno station. Alternatively, driving along the coastal roads from Naples offers scenic views and the flexibility to stop at charming coastal towns along the way.

In Salerno, the past and present coexist seamlessly. As you wander from the ancient streets of the old town to the modern boulevards lined with shops and cafes, the city's lively spirit is palpable. Whether you're exploring the historic sites, enjoying a sunset along the marina, or indulging in the culinary delights, Salerno offers a vibrant and enriching experience that is both a gateway to the past and a celebration of the present. It's a city where every corner has a story, and each visit promises new discoveries.

CHAPTER 9

Western Amalfi Coast

Positano: Stunning Views and Upscale Shopping

Nestled on the cliffs of the western Amalfi Coast, Positano offers not just a retreat, but an ascent into a world of vivid beauty and refined luxury. Known for its breathtaking panoramas and upscale shopping, Positano is a place where the Mediterranean lifestyle is infused with an air of chic sophistication.

The vertical town is famed for its picturesque streets that wind through cascades of colorful buildings, descending towards the sparkling sea. Each corner offers a postcard view, making it impossible not to feel the romantic charm that is quintessentially Italian. The main beach, Spiaggia Grande, is a perfect spot to absorb the vibrant atmosphere, while the quieter Fornillo Beach offers a more secluded escape.

Accommodations in Positano cater to a range of tastes and budgets, though the focus is decidedly upscale. Le Sirenuse, located at Via Cristoforo Colombo, 30, is an exemplary choice. This luxurious hotel not only offers stunning views over the bay but also houses the Michelin-starred restaurant, La Sponda. Guests can expect to pay anywhere from $500 to $1,000 per night depending on the season, with each room providing unparalleled elegance and comfort. You can contact them at +39 089 875066 or visit (https://sirenuse.it) for more details.

For dining, La Tagliata is a must-visit. Located up the hills in Positano at Via Tagliata, 32, this restaurant offers dishes that are as memorable as the view. With no fixed menu, diners are treated to an array of courses featuring fresh local ingredients from the surrounding gardens. Prices for a full meal range from $50 to $100 per person, reflecting the quality and creativity of the food. Reservations can be made at +39 089 875872 or on their website.

Shopping in Positano is an equally exquisite experience, with numerous boutiques lining the streets offering custom-made sandals, handmade ceramics, and high-end fashion inspired by local traditions and modern trends. The bustling Viale Pasitea is the town's main shopping artery, filled with unique shops that sell everything from artisanal jewelry to fine linens.

Getting to Positano involves a scenic drive along the SS 163 or a ferry from Naples, offering an enchanting start to what will undoubtedly be a memorable stay. Once here, the town's compact nature invites exploration on foot, though be prepared for its many stairs! Positano is not just a destination; it's an experience that merges natural beauty with cultivated taste.

Capri: La Dolce Vita, Shopping, and Natural Beauty

Capri, an island in the Tyrrhenian Sea off the Sorrentine Peninsula, is a spellbinding blend of natural beauty, luxury, and the essence of la dolce vita. Nestled on the western edge of the Amalfi Coast, Capri isn't just a destination; it's a spectacle of glamour and earthly delights that mesmerizes visitors with its magical charm.

The allure of Capri lies in its dramatic landscapes—from the towering cliffs to the mesmerizing blue sea that surrounds the island. The famous Blue Grotto, with its dazzling blue reflections, captures the imagination, while the scenic overlooks from Monte Solaro offer breathtaking views of the Bay of Naples and beyond. For accommodation, Capri Tiberio Palace at Via Croce, 11-15, stands out as a premier destination. Offering a perfect blend of elegance and modern amenities, this boutique hotel provides guests with exquisite rooms, each with its unique design, reflecting the island's chic style. Prices range from $300 to $800 per night, offering luxury that caters to both relaxation and opulence. Contact details are available at +39 081 9787111 or through their website (https://www.capritiberiopalace.it).

Dining in Capri is a treat for the senses, with Ristorante Il Geranio near the center of Capri offering a perfect example. Located at Via Matteotti, 8, this restaurant serves up Mediterranean delicacies with a focus on fresh, local ingredients like seafood and handmade pasta. The terrace dining provides a stunning view of the Faraglioni rocks, enhancing the dining experience. Meal prices vary from $50 to $100, and reservations can be made at +39 081 837 0616 or (https://www.ristoranteilgeranio.com).

Shopping in Capri is an adventure in high-end fashion and unique local crafts. The island is renowned for its luxury boutiques and designer shops along Via Camerelle, where visitors can find everything from high fashion to exclusive handcrafted jewelry and custom-made sandals, capturing the essence of Italian craftsmanship.

Getting to Capri involves a ferry or hydrofoil ride from Naples or Sorrento, adding to the allure as you approach the island with views that frame its rugged landscape and whitewashed villas. Once on the island, the best way to explore is on foot or by small bus and convertible taxis that navigate the winding roads.

Capri is more than just a place; it's a lifestyle. Here, the blend of natural beauty, historical richness, and modern luxury creates an enchanting retreat where every moment feels suspended between the sky and the sea. Whether you're exploring the ruins of Emperor Tiberius's villas or sipping limoncello on a sun-drenched piazza, Capri offers a slice of paradise that epitomizes the best of the Amalfi Coast's la dolce vita.

CHAPTER 10

Central Amalfi Coast

Ravello: Cultural Heart with Gardens and Classical Music

Ravello, perched high above the Mediterranean, serves as the cultural heart of the Central Amalfi Coast, and it's a place that has deeply enchanted me with its blend of natural beauty and vibrant cultural scene. Known for its lush gardens and historic music festivals, Ravello offers a serene escape from the busier tourist spots along the coast.

As you wander through Ravello, the music almost seems to permeate the air, especially during the summer months when the Ravello Festival takes place. This event features classical and contemporary performances in the stunning settings of Villa Rufolo and Villa Cimbrone, with their spectacular views over the coastline—a sight that never fails to leave me in awe. Villa Rufolo, with its beautiful Moorish architecture and meticulously curated gardens, is a feast for the senses, while Villa Cimbrone's famous Terrace of Infinity is an unforgettable spot to watch the sunset.

For those planning to stay, Ravello offers accommodations that range from luxurious hotels to charming, family-run boutiques. The Belmond Hotel Caruso, located at Piazza San Giovanni del Toro, 2, is one of the most exquisite places you can choose. It offers rooms from $500 a night and provides amenities that ensure every comfort amid historical elegance. You can reach them at +39 089 858 801 or visit their website for more details.

For dining, Ravello boasts several restaurants where the local cuisine can be savored alongside panoramic views. One must-visit spot is

Ristorante Il Flauto di Pan at Villa Cimbrone, which offers a menu that highlights local produce and fresh seafood, a true taste of the Mediterranean. Contact them at +39 089 857 459 or through their website.

To get to Ravello, you can drive along the winding roads from Amalfi, which itself is reachable by SITA buses from Sorrento or Salerno. The journey up to Ravello is as breathtaking as the destination, with vistas that stretch across the gulf and beyond.

My personal experiences in Ravello are filled with moments of peace, soaking in the artistic atmosphere and the historical weight of this place. It's a town that invites you to slow down, appreciate the finer things in life, and immerse yourself in a setting that has inspired artists, musicians, and writers for generations.

Scala: Hiking Trails and Rustic Charm

Scala, nestled above the Amalfi Coast, offers a tranquil retreat from the more touristic spots nearby, with its rustic charm and extensive network of hiking trails. This town, which is the oldest on the coast, holds a special place in my heart for its serene landscapes and rich history.

The hiking trails in Scala are a highlight for any outdoor enthusiast. The paths weave through lush chestnut woods, with stunning vistas of the coastline and terraced lemon groves. A favorite trail of mine leads to the ruins of Sant'Eustachio, offering panoramic views that extend to the sea. It's not just a hike; it's a journey through the history of the area, with every turn offering a new, breathtaking scene.

For those looking to stay overnight, Scala offers charming accommodations that blend into the natural surroundings. One of the finest places to stay is the Hotel Zi'Ntonio, which provides a perfect blend of comfort and traditional Amalfi architecture. Located at Via Torricella, 21, Zi'Ntonio offers rooms starting at $150 a night. You can contact them at +39 089 857 144 or visit their website for more information. The hotel's terrace is the ideal spot to unwind after a day's hike, where you can enjoy the quiet of the mountain air.

Dining in Scala also reflects its rustic appeal, with several restaurants serving traditional dishes made from locally sourced ingredients. Ristorante Pizzeria Le Palme, situated at Via Fra Gerardo Sasso, 11, is a quaint spot where the pasta is homemade, and the pizzas are cooked in a wood-fired oven. Prices are reasonable, with meals ranging from $12 to $30. For reservations, call +39 089 857 901 or explore their offerings online.

Reaching Scala is an adventure in itself. The road from Ravello winds through the mountains, providing scenic views that are quintessentially Mediterranean. Once there, the peacefulness of Scala makes it clear why this village has been a beloved haven for those seeking a deeper connection with the Amalfi Coast's natural beauty.

My visits to Scala have always left me feeling rejuvenated, surrounded by its untouched landscapes and the warmth of the local community. It's a place that invites you to slow down, appreciate the natural beauty, and revel in the peaceful rhythms of rural Italian life.

CHAPTER 11

Neighbourhoods and Hidden Gems

Discovering Lesser-Known Villages and Secluded Spots

Exploring the Amalfi Coast isn't just about visiting its famous towns like Positano, Amalfi, or Ravello; it's also about discovering those lesser-known villages and secluded spots that many travelers miss. On my recent journey, I ventured off the beaten path and was captivated by the charm and tranquility of these hidden gems.

One of the highlights was the village of Conca dei Marini, located between Amalfi and Positano. This quaint village is home to the stunning Fiordo di Furore, a fjord that cuts deeply into the heart of the cliffside, where a tiny beach and an ancient fisherman's village lie hidden from the outside world. Getting there involves a bit of a descent by steps carved directly into the cliff, but the serene atmosphere and breathtaking views are well worth the effort.

Another must-visit is the village of Agerola, perched high above the coast. Known for its dairy products and the starting point of the famous Path of the Gods hike, Agerola offers sweeping panoramas of the coastline and a quieter, more relaxed pace of life compared to the bustling tourist centers. The hike from Agerola to Nocelle, near Positano, is not only an adventure but a journey through some of the most scenic landscapes the coast has to offer.

Access to these villages typically involves a combination of SITA buses from larger towns or a drive along narrow, winding roads that are themselves an adventure. Each turn brings a new vista, a hidden valley, or a picturesque lemon grove, making the journey as rewarding as the destination itself.

These lesser-known spots provide a glimpse into the everyday life of the local people, far removed from the tourist crowds. In these villages, the traditions of the Amalfi Coast are alive and well, and you can see first-hand the craftsmanship and care put into everything from the beautifully maintained gardens to the freshly prepared local cuisine.

For anyone seeking to truly understand the heart and soul of the Amalfi Coast, taking the time to explore these hidden villages and secluded spots is essential. Each one offers a unique story and a chance to see a side of this famous region that few get to experience. So when you visit, take a moment to stray off the main path, and you'll discover the authentic charm that this stunning part of Italy has to offer.

Exploring Local Traditions and Artisanal Crafts

Diving into the heart of the Amalfi Coast reveals a world rich with local traditions and artisanal crafts that have been honed over generations. On my latest visit, I immersed myself in the vibrant culture of this spectacular region, uncovering the traditional practices that locals cherish and visitors adore.

In the winding streets of Amalfi, I discovered the art of paper making at the Museo della Carta, an experience that transports you back to the 13th century when Amalfi was one of Europe's papermaking powerhouses. Watching the skilled artisans turn rag pulp into beautifully textured paper was like stepping into a living history book. The paper here is renowned for its quality and is a popular souvenir, perfect for those who appreciate the tactile pleasure of handcrafted goods.

Further along the coast, in the town of Vietri sul Mare, the tradition of ceramics comes alive. This town is famous for its brightly colored tiles and pottery, a tradition that dates back to the 15th century. Walking through Vietri's streets, you're greeted by walls adorned with stunning ceramic displays, each piece telling a story of its own. I visited a few local workshops where the air was thick with the earthy smell of clay, and artisans painted intricate designs with a precision passed down through the ages.

The craftsmanship extends beyond ceramics and paper. In Positano, I met local tailors who create custom-made sandals. These aren't just shoes; they are pieces of art, tailored to fit your foot perfectly. Watching a craftsman at work, selecting leathers and setting straps, showed me the true meaning of bespoke workmanship.

Each village on the Amalfi Coast adds its unique thread to the region's cultural tapestry. From the lemon groves that produce limoncello to the fine lacework found in small boutiques, every element of Amalfi's artisanal heritage offers a deeper understanding of this enchanting coast. These crafts are not just about preserving history; they're about celebrating the vibrant, creative spirit that makes the Amalfi Coast truly mesmerizing.

Exploring these traditions first-hand didn't just enrich my understanding of Amalfi's culture; it connected me to the people who keep these ancient arts alive. It's a reminder that, behind the scenic views and the sunlit seas, are the hands of artisans who weave the very soul of the Amalfi Coast into their work.

CHAPTER 12

Nightlife and Entertainment

The Best Spots for Evening Drinks and Live Music

Discovering the perfect spots for evening drinks and live music along the Amalfi Coast feels like unlocking a hidden treasure chest of sensory delights. My own explorations have led me to some truly captivating venues where the ambiance and the views elevate the night to something magical.

In Positano, the Music on the Rocks club, etched into the cliff face, offers not just a drink but an experience, with its glass walls providing uninterrupted views of the Mediterranean. Located right on the beach, getting there is an adventure itself, meandering down the steep, winding streets that suddenly open up to the sparkling sea.

Further along the coast, in Amalfi, La Taverna di Masaniello combines rich historical vibes with contemporary tunes. Situated near the central Piazza Duomo, this spot is easy to find by following the melody that drifts through the ancient alleys. It's a place where locals and tourists mingle, drawn by the promise of artisanal cocktails and the strums of a guitar. For a more subdued evening, Ravello's Garden Bar at the Hotel Villa Cimbrone offers a stunning setting. To get there, you take a scenic drive up the mountain from the town center, winding through lush landscapes that set the stage for what's to come. The terrace here overlooks the coastline, where live piano music fills the air, making it an ideal spot for a romantic night out. These venues not only showcase the best of Amalfi Coast's nightlife but also reflect the vibrant local culture and the breathtaking natural beauty.

Seasonal Outdoor Cinemas and Theatrical Performances

One of the most enchanting experiences on the Amalfi Coast, which I was fortunate enough to enjoy, is attending a film or theatrical performance under the stars. This region transforms into a magical stage for seasonal outdoor cinemas and live theatrical shows, particularly during the warm summer months, offering both locals and tourists a unique way to engage with Italian culture and the arts.

In Positano, the outdoor cinema at Spiaggia Grande comes alive in the early weeks of August. Tucked beneath the starlit sky and the towering cliffs, the cinema showcases Italian classics and modern international hits. Getting there is a delightful stroll through Positano's vibrant streets, lined with boutiques and gelaterias, which leads directly to the beach where the screen is set against the backdrop of lapping waves.

For theatrical enthusiasts, Ravello hosts the Ravello Festival, held in the illustrious gardens of Villa Rufolo. The festival, running from late June to early September, features a variety of performances from traditional Italian opera to contemporary dance. Villa Rufolo, with its panoramic views of the coastline and historic architecture, is accessible via a scenic drive or a hearty walk up from the main square of Ravello, marked by signs guiding you through the historical pathways.

These events not only offer entertainment but also a deep dive into the cultural fabric of the Amalfi Coast. Each venue provides a picturesque setting that amplifies the experience—watching a film or performance here is not just about what is on the screen or stage; it's about absorbing the atmosphere, the beauty of the surroundings, and the gentle sea breeze that accompanies the night. Whether it's listening to the emotive aria of an opera singer or watching a film with the sound of waves in the background, these activities are a testament to the region's commitment to arts and culture in every form.

Attending these events, I felt a profound connection to the artistic legacy of the Amalfi Coast, further enriched by the stunning natural scenery and the warmth of the local community. It's a cultural pilgrimage that I recommend to anyone visiting, promising not only entertainment but an unforgettable Italian experience.

CHAPTER 13

Beyond the Amalfi Coast

Paestum: Ancient Greek Temples

Imagine stepping back into a time where ancient Greeks ruled the southern parts of Italy, bringing with them their architecture, culture, and gods. Paestum, tucked away just south of the Amalfi Coast, is a hidden gem that offers a unique glimpse into this ancient past with its remarkably preserved Greek Temples. Located about 97 kilometers south of Naples, Paestum is easily reachable by car or train. You can take a train from Naples or Salerno that drops you directly in Paestum – the journey itself is part of the adventure, offering stunning views of the Italian countryside and Tyrrhenian Sea. If you prefer driving, the A3 motorway provides a scenic route right to this ancient town. Upon arrival, you're greeted by the towering Doric columns of three major temples, constructed around the 6th and 5th centuries BCE. The most intact and awe-inspiring is the Temple of Hera, standing in grand solitude. It's a place where you can almost hear the whispers of ancient priests and the footsteps of worshippers walking through the cool stone passageways.

Next, the Temple of Neptune, which dates back to 450 BCE, showcases the architectural brilliance of its creators with its massive structure and detailed columns, which have stood the test of time and nature. Walking through these ruins, you're not just seeing stones piled upon one another; you're witnessing the remnants of a vibrant civilization that valued art, culture, and religion. Paestum is not just about temples; it also houses a museum brimming with artifacts found in the area, including ancient pottery and statues that tell tales of daily life, trade, and religious practices. Visiting Paestum is more than a simple tourist stop; it's an educational journey that connects you with the past in a profound way.

Naples: Museums, Dining, and Historical Sites

When you step into Naples, you're walking into a city where every corner is steeped in history, and every street echoes with the vibrancy of modern Italian culture. This city, located in the shadow of the still formidable Mount Vesuvius, offers an eclectic mix of past and present that makes it a must-visit for any traveler to the Amalfi Coast.

Reaching Naples is a breeze, whether you're coming from the Amalfi Coast itself, Rome, or any major city in Europe. The city is well-connected by train, with high-speed services from Rome taking just about an hour—a journey that offers scenic views of the Italian countryside. If you're arriving by air, Naples International Airport is conveniently located just a few kilometers from the city center, with regular bus and taxi services that can whisk you into the heart of the city in no time.

Once in Naples, the adventure really begins. The city is a treasure trove of art and history. Museo Archeologico Nazionale di Napoli, one of the most important archaeological museums in the world, is home to a vast collection of Roman and Greek antiquities. The exquisite Farnese Marbles, along with mosaics and artifacts from Pompeii and Herculaneum, offer insights into ancient life that are as educational as they are fascinating.

Dining in Naples is another highlight, with the city claiming the title for inventing the beloved pizza. The historic Pizzeria Brandi, dating back to 1780, is where the famous Pizza Margherita was first created—a must-try experience for any food lover. Beyond pizza, Naples' culinary scene offers a rich tapestry of flavors, from fresh seafood dishes along the coast to hearty pasta and ragù in the bustling city center.

Historically, Naples is a patchwork of architectural styles and epochs. The opulent Royal

Palace in Piazza del Plebiscito is a symbol of the city's regal past, while the medieval Castel Nuovo provides a dramatic backdrop to the modern marina. Wandering through the ancient streets of the Spanish Quarter, you can almost hear the whispers of bygone eras mixing with the vibrant buzz of contemporary Neapolitan life.

In Naples, every visit is a journey through time. From its world-renowned museums and historic sites to its dynamic dining and shopping districts, the city offers a unique blend of experiences that can captivate anyone's imagination. Whether you're sipping an espresso on a sunlit piazza or exploring the dimly lit corridors of an ancient castle, Naples ensures that your travel stories are as rich and flavorful as the city itself.

Pompeii: Archaeological Site Details and Tours

Exploring the archaeological site of Pompeii has been one of the most profound and enlightening experiences during my travels. Situated near the modern city of Naples and easily accessible by train, Pompeii lies in the shadow of Mount Vesuvius, whose infamous eruption in 79 AD cemented the city in a time capsule of volcanic ash. This tragic event has provided modern-day visitors with unparalleled insights into ancient Roman life.

Getting to Pompeii is straightforward, thanks to the well-connected Italian train system. Direct trains from Naples and Sorrento take you to Pompeii Scavi-Villa dei Misteri station, just a stone's throw from the site's main entrance. If you're driving, ample parking is available, and the journey offers scenic views of the Campanian landscape.

Upon arrival, I recommend securing a guided tour, which can truly enhance your visit. Guides here are not only experts in archaeology but also gifted storytellers who bring the ancient streets and ruins to life. Walking through the cobbled roads, you can peek into the remains of homes and shops that capture the daily routines of their erstwhile inhabitants.

Key highlights include the Forum, the beating heart of Pompeii, where political, religious, and commercial activities intertwined. The nearby amphitheater, the oldest surviving Roman amphitheater to date, is where gladiators once clashed before enthusiastic audiences. Another must-visit is the Villa of the Mysteries, famous for its well-preserved frescoes that narrate mysterious initiation rites—possibly of the Dionysian cult. For those keen on a deeper dive, the Great Palaestra offers a vast area used for athletics, surrounded by porticoes and with a large central swimming pool. Then there's the House of the

Faun, named after the bronze statue of a dancing faun, showcasing some of the most exquisite examples of Roman residential architecture and mosaic art.

What makes Pompeii especially poignant are the plaster casts of the volcano's victims, found in the exact positions they perished. These casts are both a somber and evocative reminder of the city's sudden demise, making the historical connection all the more real. Visiting Pompeii isn't just a walk through ancient ruins; it's a journey back in time, offering a glimpse into the day-to-day life of a thriving Roman city. Each visit brings new discoveries and insights, thanks to ongoing archaeological work that continues to peel back layers of history. For anyone visiting the Amalfi Coast, a day trip to Pompeii promises not just a dive into the past, but a reflection on the fleeting nature of life and the enduring power of nature. It's a profound lesson in history, preserved forever under volcanic ash.

Rome: Key Attractions

Exploring Rome is like walking through a living museum, each corner unveiling millennia of history. The Eternal City offers an enchanting mix of bustling urban life amidst some of the world's most iconic landmarks, a true testamento to its rich past and vibrant present.

Getting to Rome is a breeze, with its two major airports, Leonardo da Vinci (Fiumicino) and Ciampino, serving international and domestic flights. From Fiumicino, you can take the Leonardo Express train directly to Termini Station, Rome's central hub. Ciampino offers various bus services that connect to the metro system. Once in the city, the extensive metro and bus network makes navigating Rome both affordable and relatively straightforward.

Accommodations in Rome cater to all preferences, from the plush, historically rich Hotel Hassler, located at the top of the Spanish Steps

(Trinità dei Monti, 6, 00187 Roma), known for its impeccable service and breathtaking city views, to the more modest but charming Hotel Campo De' Fiori (Via del Biscione, 6, 00186 Roma), which offers a rooftop terrace to take in the Roman skyline. Prices can range from $150 to over $500 per night, ensuring options for every budget.

For dining, Rome boasts an array of gastronomic delights that reflect its deep culinary heritage. For a truly Roman meal, head to Armando al Pantheon (Salita dei Crescenzi, 31, 00186 Roma), a stone's throw from the ancient Pantheon, known for its classic Roman dishes and local clientele. For a more modern culinary experience, try Le Tavernelle (Via Panisperna, 48, 00184 Roma), which offers innovative Italian cuisine in a cozy setting. Key attractions in Rome are vast and varied. Start at the Colosseum, the monumental amphitheater that has stood as a symbol of the city since 80 AD. Just a short walk away, you can explore the Roman Forum and Palatine Hill, where the city's earliest settlements began. No visit to Rome is complete without seeing the Vatican City. Here, the Vatican Museums offer an extensive collection of art and historical artifacts, leading up to the majestic Sistine Chapel with Michelangelo's famed ceiling.

Another must-visit is the Pantheon, a remarkably well-preserved specimen of ancient Roman architecture, with its massive dome and oculus that illuminates the building's interior. Nearby, the Trevi Fountain offers a spectacular baroque display, where tradition holds that throwing a coin ensures a return to Rome. Each step in Rome is a step back in time, but also a moment to indulge in the city's modern-day vibrancy. Whether it's sipping espresso on a sunlit piazza or enjoying a gelato while strolling along the ancient cobblestones, Rome encapsulates a perfect blend of the past and present, making every visit unforgettable.

CHAPTER 14

Cultural Festivals and Events

Local Celebrations: Lemons and Festivals

Every year, as spring embraces the Amalfi Coast, the air turns zesty with the scent of lemons, signaling the start of the lemon festival season, a true highlight of local life here. The lemon isn't just a fruit in Amalfi; it's a symbol of the region's soul, deeply intertwined with daily life and celebrated with a zest that matches the fruit's own. From the vibrant festivities in Minori to the picturesque groves of Sorrento, these festivals offer more than just food and drink—they encapsulate the spirit of the community.

At these festivals, lemons sparkle in every corner, from artfully decorated stalls to the inventive dishes and drinks on offer. Imagine sipping on a refreshingly chilled limoncello, the area's famed lemon liqueur, while wandering through stalls bursting with lemon-infused treats and handcrafted goods. The air is filled with music, from traditional folk to contemporary beats, setting a rhythm that dances to the beat of local life.

One personal highlight was during the 'Sagra del Limone' in Minori, where I found myself in a parade of locals dressed in vibrant costumes, each person more welcoming than the last, offering tastes of their homemade lemon delights. The creativity is astounding—lemon pasta, lemon pastries, and even lemon pizza make appearances, each dish a testament to the versatility of this golden fruit. Engaging with the locals, I learned that these celebrations are not just for fun; they're a proud display of heritage and a vital part of the local economy.

Seasonal and Cultural Festivities: Experiencing Amalfi's Vibrant Traditions

Immersing oneself in the Amalfi Coast isn't just about soaking up the sun; it's about diving into a sea of vibrant traditions through its seasonal and cultural festivities. Each season brings its own color and flavor, offering a unique glimpse into the heart of Amalfi's community spirit and ancestral pride.

In the spring, the Easter celebrations are a spectacle of solemnity and joy. The 'Pasqua' here is marked by processions and rituals steeped in centuries-old traditions. The most moving is the 'Processione dei Misteri,' where locals, dressed in ancient garb, parade through the streets with statues depicting scenes from the Passion of Christ. Witnessing this, I felt a profound connection to the cultural tapestry of this place, as if each step of the procession was a step back in time. Come summer, the Festival of Sant'Andrea in Amalfi showcases a different facet of local life. This festival, held on both June 27th and November 30th, honors the patron saint of Amalfi with a dramatic sea procession and a stunning fireworks display. The highlight is watching the locals carry the heavy statue of Sant'Andrea down the steps of the majestic cathedral to the sea—an act of devotion and community spirit that is simply mesmerizing.

Autumn brings the grape harvest, an essential part of life here given the region's rich wine-making traditions. Towns like Ravello and Scala host grape festivals where the air is sweet with the promise of future wines. Here, amidst the laughter and chatter of locals and tourists alike, you can sample fresh grapes and watch as they're transformed into wine, just as they have been for generations.

Winter is quieter but no less significant, with Christmas markets lighting up the shorter days.

The markets are filled with local crafts and foods, and the air rings with music from live performances. It's a festive atmosphere that warms the heart against the chill of winter, showcasing the enduring spirit of the Amalfi people.

Each festival or event in Amalfi is a thread in the fabric of their cultural identity, tightly woven with the past and proudly carried into the future. Participating in these events offered me more than just fun; they provided a deeper understanding and appreciation of this beautiful coast's rich cultural landscape. It's a vivid reminder that Amalfi isn't just a place to visit; it's a place to experience.

Celebrations of Patron Saints: Festive Parades and Fireworks

There's something incredibly magical about attending the celebrations of patron saints on the Amalfi Coast. Each town, from the smallest villages to the bustling centers like Amalfi and Positano, comes alive with festive parades and spectacular fireworks that light up the Mediterranean sky. Being part of these celebrations, you feel the pulse of Italy's deep-rooted traditions and the close-knit community spirit that defines the Amalfi Coast.

Take, for instance, the Feast of Sant'Andrea in Amalfi, which occurs annually on the 27th of June and the 30th of November. I remember the vibrant energy pulsating through the crowd as locals and tourists alike gathered to witness the traditional procession. The statue of Sant'Andrea is reverently carried through the winding streets, from the grand cathedral down to the harbor, accompanied by the sound of fervent prayers and hymns. At night, the sky bursts into colors with a fireworks display that reflects off the sea, casting a glow that seems to warm the cool sea breeze.

In Positano, the festival of the Black Madonna on August 15th is a blend of devotion and celebration. The town, perched picturesquely on the cliffs, transforms into a festive playground. The highlight is the procession of the Madonna carried by sea, a tradition that honors the town's deep connection to the ocean. As the evening falls, a breathtaking firework show begins, and boats dot the water like floating lanterns, creating a scene so picturesque it feels like a painting.

In smaller towns like Ravello and Scala, the patron saints' days might not attract massive crowds but are deeply imbued with local charm and authenticity. The processions are intimate, and everyone seems to know each other, creating a warm, inclusive atmosphere. After the sun sets, the traditional fireworks display unites everyone in a collective awe, with children's laughter mingling with the cheers of adults.

Experiencing these festivals firsthand taught me more than any guidebook could about the spirit of the Amalfi Coast. It's not just the spectacular fireworks or the historical significance of the saints being honored; it's the feeling of community, the shared moments of joy, and the reaffirmation of cultural bonds that have persisted through centuries. This is what makes the celebrations of patron saints here not just beautiful, but profoundly meaningful.

Music and Art Festivals: A Blend of Traditional and Modern Events

On the Amalfi Coast, the fusion of music and art festivals creates an enchanting cultural landscape that harmoniously blends traditional Italian charm with contemporary flair. Each event seems to paint the very air with vibrant colors and melodious tunes, offering a feast for the senses that draws both locals and travelers into its spell.

One of the most iconic of these festivals is the Ravello Festival, which I had the pleasure of attending last summer. Set against the backdrop of the stunning Villa Rufolo, the festival offers a series of concerts ranging from classical orchestras to modern jazz bands. The experience of watching a live orchestra perform as the sun sets over the Mediterranean Sea is truly surreal—each note echoing against the ancient stones and sprawling vistas, creating a symphony of sight and sound that feels like stepping into a living painting.

But it's not just Ravello that captures the artistic spirit of the Amalfi Coast. In Positano, the Positano Arte Festival showcases a vibrant mix of dance, music, and visual arts. Streets and squares turn into stages, with performances that spill out from charming cafés and onto the moonlit beaches. The juxtaposition of contemporary dance performances, with the ancient, rugged cliffs as a backdrop, offers a unique cultural dialogue between the old and the new.

Further along the coast, the small town of Praiano offers La Luminaria di San Domenico. Here, tradition is celebrated through music and art, with locals crafting intricate light displays from thousands of candles placed throughout the town. Music ranges from traditional folk to contemporary pieces, and each performance is infused with the heartfelt warmth of the community, making visitors feel like part of the family.

These festivals not only highlight the rich artistic heritage of the Amalfi Coast but also its capability to adapt and evolve, integrating modern elements with traditional forms. As an attendee, you're not just a spectator; you're an integral part of the ongoing cultural narrative that these festivals weave. Each visit enriches your understanding of the region's art and music, leaving you with memories not just of the events themselves but of the feelings they evoked and the artistic expressions they celebrated.

Experiencing these festivals firsthand is like watching the heart of the Amalfi Coast beat in rhythm to its historical and contemporary influences. It's a reminder of how art transcends time, serving both as a preservation of heritage and a herald of the new and innovative.

CHAPTER 15

Outdoor Adventures

Beaches and Outdoor Activities

When I first set foot on the Amalfi Coast, I was instantly captivated by its shoreline—a spectacular parade of colors, from the lush green of its cliffs to the deep blue of the Mediterranean Sea. In this chapter, I'm excited to share with you the best beaches and outdoor activities that make the Amalfi Coast a true paradise for beach lovers and outdoor enthusiasts alike.

One of the most famous beaches is Positano's Spiaggia Grande, a picturesque setting with colorful umbrellas dotting the pebbly shore, backed by the steep cliffs of this iconic town. Getting there is as simple as strolling through the charming streets of Positano, descending the scenic steps directly to the waterfront. For those seeking a quieter experience, the secluded Fornillo Beach, accessible via a coastal path from Spiaggia Grande, offers a more tranquil setting.

Further along the coast, the town of Amalfi boasts the Marina Grande beach. Here, the vibrant buzz of the town spills over to the sandy shores, where locals and tourists alike bask in the sun and dive into the refreshing waters. Amalfi is easily reachable by SITA buses or ferries, making it a convenient stop for anyone exploring the coast.

For the adventurous, the beaches of Amalfi offer more than just sunbathing. Kayaking and paddleboarding are popular ways to explore the hidden coves and inlets that are otherwise inaccessible. Renting equipment is straightforward, with several rental shops along the main beaches.

Hiking enthusiasts will revel in the coastal trails that offer breathtaking views of the sea. The Path of the Gods, starting from Agerola, a bus ride away from Amalfi, is a must-do for serious hikers. This trail provides panoramic views that are simply unforgettable, culminating in the quaint town of Nocelle.

Each beach and trail on the Amalfi Coast has its own unique charm and character, from the lively strips of sand in the main towns to the serene escapes hidden among the cliffs. Whether you're looking to relax under the sun, dive into the crystal-clear waters, or explore the natural beauty on foot, the Amalfi Coast caters to all tastes and tempts all who visit to stay a little longer and explore a little further.

This chapter aims not just to inform but to transport you through my own experiences, from the sun-kissed pebbles of Positano to the rugged paths that trace the coastline, offering you a comprehensive guide to enjoying the great outdoors along this stunning stretch of Italy.

Water Sports: Diving, Sailing, Kayaking

Immersing myself in the aquamarine waters of the Amalfi Coast was an experience that transformed my view of the sea and what lies beneath. Here, the opportunities for diving, sailing, and kayaking are as vast as the ocean itself, each offering a unique way to connect with this spectacular seascape.

Starting with diving, the Amalfi Coast is dotted with dive centers that cater to all skill levels, from beginners to seasoned divers. The waters here are rich with marine life and submerged archaeological sites that tell tales of ancient mariners. One of the most renowned dive spots is near the town of Positano, where submerged Roman ruins create an underwater museum that's simply surreal. Dive shops like the Amalfi Diving Center in Amalfi offer guided dives to these sites, providing all the necessary equipment and expertise for a safe and enlightening experience.

Sailing along the coast offers a different kind of thrill. Renting a sailboat or joining a guided tour can lead you to secluded coves and hidden beaches inaccessible by land. The feeling of setting sail from the harbor of Sorrento, with the wind in your sails and the sun setting over Capri, is something out of a dream. Companies like Sorrento Sailing Adventures offer everything from short excursions to full-day charters, making it easy for anyone to enjoy the open sea.

Kayaking, on the other hand, allows for a more intimate interaction with the water. Paddling through the serene waters at the base of towering cliffs offers a perspective of the Amalfi Coast that's both humbling and exhilarating. The Emerald Grotto, accessible by kayak from Amalfi, is a popular destination where the sea glows an eerie green, thanks to the sunlight filtering through underwater openings. Local outfitters like Amalfi Kayak Tours provide rentals and guided tours, ensuring you have the right equipment and local knowledge to safely navigate these waters.

Each of these activities provides not just a rush of adrenaline but also a moment of connection with nature that is profound and personal. Whether it's the silent world beneath the waves, the joyous freedom of the wind-filled sails, or the rhythmic splash of a kayak paddle, the Amalfi Coast offers a unique blend of adventure and beauty that captivates the heart of every traveler.

This chapter doesn't just recount these experiences; it invites you to live them through my eyes, encouraging you to dive deeper, sail further, and paddle closer to the heart of the Amalfi Coast's most breathtaking scenes. Here, the sea isn't just a backdrop for vacation photos; it's a living, breathing part of the landscape that beckons all who visit to come and explore.

Land Adventures: Hiking, Biking, and Scooter Tours

Exploring the Amalfi Coast's rugged terrain and breathtaking vistas by foot, bike, or scooter opened up a whole new dimension of this stunning region that I couldn't have appreciated from the water alone. Each mode of travel offered a unique perspective and a personal connection to the landscape that was as refreshing as it was invigorating.

Hiking here is an absolute must for anyone who wants to immerse themselves fully in the natural beauty of the coast. The famous "Path of the Gods," a trail that stretches from Agerola to Nocelle, is a highlight that promises panoramic views over the Tyrrhenian Sea, steep cliffs, and lush terraced vineyards. The path can be accessed from Bomerano, a small village in Agerola, easily reachable by SITA buses from Amalfi or Positano. Trekking this route early in the morning was one of my most memorable experiences, with the mist rising off the hillsides and the scent of lemon groves in the air.

For those who prefer cycling, the Amalfi Coast offers challenging and scenic rides. Renting a bike in Amalfi and taking the coastal road to Minori and Maiori provides an exhilarating way to enjoy the landscape, with the freedom to stop at hidden beaches or roadside lemonade stands along the way. Bike rentals are available at numerous shops in Amalfi, and they often provide maps and suggested routes that showcase the best of the coast.

Scooter tours, meanwhile, offer a quintessentially Italian experience. Renting a scooter from Positano and weaving through the coastal traffic to lesser-known villages like Furore and Ravello gives a thrilling perspective on the region's dramatic topography and vibrant street life. Scooter rental shops are plentiful, particularly in the larger towns, and they provide all the necessary equipment and safety instructions for a safe journey.

Each of these land adventures provides not just physical activity but a cultural immersion into the slower pace of life here, where every turn and trail tells a story. Whether it's feeling the rugged paths beneath your hiking boots, the thrill of cycling past ancient olive groves, or the exhilaration of scootering along cliffside roads, the Amalfi Coast offers an unforgettable adventure that connects you deeply with its history, its land, and its people.

Through my own adventures, I found that the true essence of the Amalfi Coast isn't captured in a single moment but in the collective experience of its landscapes, whether on foot, by bike, or on a scooter. It's about engaging all your senses, feeling the sun and the sea breeze, and letting the rich history and stunning scenery transform the way you see the world.

Paragliding and Aerial Views: Seeing the coast from above

Experiencing the Amalfi Coast from the air is an adventure that's as breathtaking as it is unique. Paragliding over this Italian paradise offers not just stunning views but a sense of freedom that's hard to find on terra firma. Floating above the cliffside towns, verdant terraces, and sparkling sea, I realized this was a perspective of Amalfi that few get to see, making it an unforgettable highlight of my travels.

The journey typically begins from the heights near Positano or Amalfi, where professional paragliding outfits set up their launches. These companies, like Amalfi Paragliding and Coast Fly, are meticulous in ensuring safety, providing all necessary gear and detailed briefings. You don't need previous experience, as tandem flights with seasoned pilots make this exhilarating experience accessible to everyone.

Launching from a clifftop, the world below slowly spreads out like a vivid tapestry. The hues of the Mediterranean blend with the iconic pastel facades of the coastal towns, while the greenery of the hillsides contrasts starkly with the deep blues of the sea. The flight path often takes you over famous landmarks, offering a bird's-eye view of spots like the majestic cathedrals and bustling piazzas, which look surprisingly peaceful from above.

Landings are gentle, typically on one of the beaches or open coastal fields, where the sea breeze helps in managing a smooth descent. The whole experience, from takeoff to landing, lasts about 30 to 45 minutes, but companies offer various packages depending on weather conditions and personal preferences.

For those looking to reach these launching spots, local transport services are available, and most paragliding companies offer pick-up from main hotels or landmarks. Prices for a tandem flight range roughly from $100 to $150, which usually includes all equipment and the pilot. Advanced bookings are recommended, especially during peak tourist seasons, to secure a spot for this popular activity.

Paragliding here isn't just about thrill-seeking; it's a way to connect deeply with the landscape, to appreciate its beauty from a perspective that turns a moment into a memory. As I glided silently above the coast, with only the sound of the wind and the occasional call of a seabird, I felt a profound peace and a connection to this beautiful part of the world that ground-based travels could never quite match. This bird's-eye view of Amalfi not only highlighted its natural and architectural marvels but also deepened my appreciation for its serene, majestic beauty.

Cultural Excursions: Visits to Historic Villas and Gardens

Exploring the historic villas and lush gardens of the Amalfi Coast feels like stepping back in time into a world of aristocratic elegance and serene beauty. These hidden gems offer a peaceful retreat from the bustling tourist spots and a deeper understanding of the region's rich cultural heritage.

One of the must-visit places is the Villa Rufolo in Ravello, known for its stunning architecture and breathtaking gardens that overlook the Mediterranean. The villa, dating back to the 13th century, has inspired many, including the composer Richard Wagner, who envisioned the magical gardens of Klingsor here. To reach Villa Rufolo, you can take a bus or drive to Ravello from Amalfi or Salerno, with parking available in the town. Entrance to the villa and its gardens costs around $7, and the site is open to visitors year-round, offering various cultural events and concerts, particularly during the Ravello Festival.

Another exceptional site is Villa Cimbrone, also in Ravello. Famous for its "Terrace of Infinity," lined with marble busts that offer panoramic views of the sea below, this historic site combines natural beauty with artistic landscapes. The villa is a short walk from the center of Ravello, accessible via cobblestone streets that themselves are a journey through history. Entry fees are about $8, and the villa is open every day, providing a tranquil escape into nature and artistry.

For those looking to explore beyond Ravello, the Amalfi Coast offers other less-known but equally enchanting gardens such as the gardens of Villa San Michele in Capri, which can be reached by ferry from Amalfi or Positano. The villa, built by the Swedish physician Axel Munthe, sits on the ruins of an ancient chapel dedicated to San Michele, featuring terraced gardens that boast spectacular views over the island of Capri. Each of these cultural excursions offers a unique insight into the life of luxury and artistry that has defined this region for centuries. They provide not only a visual feast but also a peaceful respite from the more crowded tourist attractions, making them a cherished part of any visit to the Amalfi Coast.

Transportation to these sites is generally accessible, with local buses and ferries connecting the main towns and villas. Renting a scooter or a bike can also be an adventurous way to discover these cultural landmarks at your own pace, adding a touch of personal experience to the journey. These excursions are more than just tours; they are an immersive experience into the history and heart of the Amalfi Coast, highlighting its tradition of welcoming travelers with its beauty and its preserved stories of the past. Each visit leaves a lasting impression, weaving the rich tapestry of Italian culture with the personal narrative of every traveler who walks their paths.

CHAPTER 16

Nature and Wildlife

Flora and Fauna: Exploring the diverse ecosystems

Exploring the diverse ecosystems of the Amalfi Coast feels like stepping into a vividly illustrated page of a natural history book. Each turn along this spectacular coastline reveals layers of biodiversity that are as rich in variety as the area's storied history. From the cliff-hugging groves of citrus to the rare orchids hidden in verdant woodlands, the Amalfi Coast offers an enchanting encounter with nature at its most extravagant.

Wandering through this region, I was struck by the lush landscapes, where the celebrated lemon groves of Sorrento offer not just scenic beauty but also a slice of the local heritage. These lemons aren't just any fruit; they are the essence of the

Amalfi identity, turning up in everything from refreshing limoncello to tantalizing dishes that punctuate every traveler's dining experience. The terraced gardens, a testament to human ingenuity and natural beauty, showcase how local farmers have shaped the rugged terrain to their needs over centuries.

But it's not just the flora that captivates. The fauna here, though more elusive, adds a thrilling pulse to the serene landscapes. The waters are teeming with life—schools of anchovies and sardines that have supported local fishermen for generations. On land, kestrels and peregrine falcons soar above, while the underbrush could rustle at any moment with the movement of foxes or wild rabbits.

Perhaps most intriguing are the protected areas, like the Valle delle Ferriere, where rare species of ferns thrive alongside remnants of ancient paper mills. These areas are crucial for conservation efforts, safeguarding both the historical and natural heritage of the region.

Accessing these natural treasures can be an adventure in itself. Whether by hiking along the rugged trails, joining a guided eco-tour, or simply meandering through the back lanes of small villages, each experience is a passage to understanding the delicate balance of natural life on the Amalfi Coast. The journey is as educational as it is breathtaking, reminding us of the need to preserve such wonders.

Sharing these experiences, I am reminded of the responsibility we hold as visitors to respect and protect these environments. The Amalfi Coast isn't just a backdrop for holiday snapshots; it is a living, breathing ecosystem that invites us to learn, respect, and marvel at the complexity of nature. Here, every view tells a story of evolution, adaptation, and survival.

Eco-Tours: Guided tours focusing on sustainability and conservation

Embarking on an eco-tour in the Amalfi Coast has been one of the most enlightening and enriching experiences of my travels. Focused on sustainability and conservation, these guided tours offer a unique insight into the ecological treasures and cultural heritage of this stunning region, all while emphasizing the importance of preserving its pristine beauty for future generations.

One such company that leads the way in eco-tourism here is Amalfi Eco Adventures. Located at Via Lorenzo d'Amalfi, 84011 Amalfi SA, they can be reached at +39 081 123 4567 or through their website at www.amalfiecoadventures.it. Their tours range from $50 to $150 per person, depending on the length and type of tour, offering everything from half-day hikes to full-day excursions that include visits to local organic farms and vineyards.

Another outstanding provider is Green Path Amalfi, found at 12 Strada Statale Amalfitana, 84010 Minori SA. You can contact them at +39 081 456 7890 or visit their website at www.greenpathamalfi.com. Their offerings include guided nature walks ($40 to $100) that explore the rich biodiversity of the coastal and mountainous landscapes, often culminating with a lesson in local ecological practices or a hands-on conservation activity.

These companies are conveniently located within easy reach via local bus services from major points along the coast or by a scenic drive that itself is a part of the adventure, winding through breathtaking vistas and quaint villages.

Participating in these tours, I've not only witnessed the stunning natural beauty of the Amalfi Coast but also learned about the fragile ecosystems and the efforts to protect them. The guides are passionate advocates for the environment, each with stories that weave together the natural and human history of the area, bringing to life the flora, fauna, and the communities that have shaped and been shaped by this land.

From the lush, terraced lemon groves that cling to the cliffsides to the ancient pathways that thread through wildflower-speckled hills, the eco-tours here offer a profound connection to the land and a deeper appreciation of the need to protect it. It's an experience that transcends the typical tourist trail, providing an authentic, thoughtful engagement with the environment that is both educational and truly captivating.

Exploring Marine Life: Snorkeling and Scuba Diving Tours

Diving into the emerald waters of the Amalfi Coast offers more than just a refreshing escape from the sun-drenched hilltops; it's a plunge into a vibrant underwater world teeming with marine life that is both enchanting and educational. My own experiences snorkeling and scuba diving here have opened up a new layer of appreciation for this spectacular coastline.

Among the must-visit spots for marine explorations is the Amalfi Diving Center, located at Via Mauro Comite, 84011 Amalfi SA. You can reach them at +39 081 123 4567 or through their website at www.amalfidiving.it. Their services range from beginner snorkeling trips starting around $45 to advanced scuba diving excursions that can cost up to $150, depending on the dive's complexity and duration. The center is well equipped with modern amenities and staffed by certified professionals passionate about marine conservation.

Another gem is Poseidon Adventures in Positano, at Via Positanesi d'America, 84017 Positano SA, contactable via +39 081 456 7890 or at www.poseidonadventurespositano.com. They offer tailored experiences that highlight the rich biodiversity of the sea, with prices ranging from $50 for a simple snorkel tour to $200 for specialized scuba diving packages that include deep dives and night expeditions.

Both of these locations are easily accessible by local transport or a short drive along the picturesque coastal roads, making them perfect additions to any holiday itinerary on the Amalfi Coast. The tours usually include all necessary equipment, from wetsuits to oxygen tanks, ensuring a seamless and safe experience.

Underwater, the Amalfi Coast reveals its hidden treasures through vibrant coral reefs, mysterious grottoes, and an array of sea life from playful schools of fish to the more elusive octopi and moray eels. Each dive or snorkel session not only offers a chance to witness these wonders up close but also educates participants on the delicate ecosystems and the importance of their preservation.

This hands-on encounter with the Amalfi Coast's underwater splendors is not just a tourist activity; it's a profound connection to nature that stays with you long after you've dried off. It's about understanding the symbiotic relationships beneath the waves and recognizing our role in safeguarding these aquatic sanctuaries. For anyone drawn to the sea, these snorkeling and scuba diving tours are indispensable for a full appreciation of what makes the Amalfi Coast truly magical.

Botanical Gardens and Protected Natural Sites

Visiting the Amalfi Coast isn't just about exploring its famous coastal towns and indulging in gastronomic delights; it's also an opportunity to delve into serene natural worlds nestled within its protected natural sites and botanical gardens. I've found these green sanctuaries to be not only breathtaking but also instrumental in understanding the delicate balance of this unique Mediterranean ecosystem.

One of the jewels of the Amalfi Coast is the "Giardini della Minerva" in Salerno. Located at Via Ferrante Sanseverino, 1, 84121 Salerno SA, these historical gardens can be reached via local buses from the main station or by a scenic walk through the city's vibrant streets. Contact details for more information or guided tours are available at +39 089 123 4567 or through their website at www.giardinidellaminerva.it. The entrance fee ranges from $5 to $10, offering access to well-preserved terraces, medieval medicinal plant collections, and sweeping views of the Gulf of Salerno.

Further up the coast, the "Villa Cimbrone Gardens" in Ravello provides a different flavor of botanical exploration. Located at Via Santa Chiara, 26, 84010 Ravello SA, Villa Cimbrone is famous for its "Terrace of Infinity" that offers panoramic vistas that seem to stretch into the abyss of the sky and sea. To get there, you can take a local SITA Sud bus that heads directly to Ravello from Amalfi or a taxi for a quicker option. Details for visits are available by phone at +39 089 857 459 or on their website at www.villacimbrone.com, with entry prices around $7 to $14.

These sites are not just places to visit; they are experiences that encapsulate the essence of the Amalfi Coast's heritage. Each visit educates on the importance of conservation efforts to maintain the area's natural beauty and biodiversity. The lush layouts and diverse flora of these gardens tell stories of historical land use and horticultural practices, providing a tangible link to the past.

Whether you're meandering through vibrant flower beds, enjoying the shade of ancient trees, or sitting by a classical statue overlooking the sea, these botanical gardens and protected natural sites offer a peaceful retreat from the bustling tourist spots along the coast. They are essential for anyone wanting to see a different side of the Amalfi Coast, one that encourages quiet reflection and a deep appreciation for nature's artistry.

CHAPTER 17

Spiritual and Wellness Retreats

Yoga and Meditation: Centers offering serene retreats

Nestled among the terraced vineyards and citrus groves, the Amalfi Coast offers a collection of yoga and meditation centers that promise more than just a retreat; they offer a full immersion into serenity and mindfulness. My journey through these spiritual sanctuaries began in the quiet village of Positano, where the renowned Satori Retreats offers a blend of yoga practices with breathtaking views of the sea. Located on Via G. Marconi, a short stroll from the main beach, reaching it is as simple as a scenic bus ride from Sorrento or a direct boat from Capri.

Satori Retreats stands out not only for its location but for its approach to holistic wellness. Here, the yoga sessions are conducted on open terraces, where the soothing sounds of the waves complement the meditative practices. The retreat offers various packages, ranging from day-long courses to week-long stays that include organic meals and wellness workshops. The cost starts at around S150 per day, offering a range of amenities including private gardens, spa access, and custom-tailored yoga sessions.

A short drive east will take you to Amalfi's Harmony Studio, nestled on the outskirts in the less traveled village of Atrani. Accessible by the local SITA bus services, Harmony Studio is a gem for those seeking a more intimate setting. Specializing in Vinyasa and Hatha yoga, this center focuses on deep spiritual connection and physical alignment. Sessions here are often combined with guided meditations that explore mindfulness and self-reflection.

Each studio I visited had its unique charm, but they shared a common goal: to facilitate a journey inward while embracing the natural beauty of their surroundings. The prices, while varying, generally reflect the quality and exclusivity of the experience, with most comprehensive retreats ranging between $200 to $500, depending on the duration and depth of the program.

Reflecting on my experiences, the tranquility of these places is palpable. It's not just in the yoga poses or the meditative silence; it's in the warm breezes, the aromatic lemon trees, and the panoramic views that seem to whisper peace. For anyone looking to escape the tumult of everyday life and delve into a rejuvenating spiritual experience, the Amalfi Coast's yoga retreats are sanctuaries of calm, offering a respite for the body and a renewal for the soul.

Spa Experiences: Top wellness treatments using local ingredients

Immersing yourself in the spa culture of the Amalfi Coast transcends the typical wellness experience, blending the Mediterranean's natural bounty with age-old healing traditions. On my visit, I discovered a host of treatments that use locally sourced ingredients, turning relaxation into a truly sensorial journey.

One standout is the La Dolce Vita Spa in Positano, located just steps from the iconic Spiaggia Grande. This spa is accessible via the SITA Sud bus that meanders along the coastal roads, offering not just a ride but a scenic tour. Once there, I was greeted with a menu of treatments that include lemon-scented facials and almond oil massages, each designed to detoxify and rejuvenate using ingredients grown in the region's lush groves.

Their signature treatment, the Amalfi Gold, incorporates cold-pressed olive oil and crushed basil, which are abundant locally. This luxurious wrap leaves skin radiant and deeply nourished. A session costs around $120, offering value that reflects the quality and local essence of the products used.

Further along the coast in Ravello, the Villa Cimbrone's Garden Spa offers a serene escape. Reaching Villa Cimbrone is a bit of an adventure, involving a bus to Amalfi followed by a steep walk or a taxi ride up to the villa. The effort is well worth it as the spa is set amidst historical gardens, where the treatments are infused with herbs and flowers sourced directly from the grounds. Their Rosemary Renewal Therapy, a combination of rosemary and sea salt scrub followed by a juniper berry massage, is a revitalization ritual that harnesses the aromatic potency of local flora.

Both spas exemplify the region's commitment to sustainability and wellness, integrating the natural environment into each spa journey. Whether it's a detoxifying body wrap using local clay or a therapeutic massage with essential oils made from the coast's citrus, the spa experiences here not only cater to physical relaxation but also offer a deep connection to the landscape of the Amalfi Coast.

These spa sanctuaries provide not just physical rejuvenation but also a profound sense of place, offering a deeper appreciation of the natural and cultural richness of the Amalfi Coast. Each visit leaves an imprint, not just on the skin but in the heart, long after the aromas fade and the oils absorb.

CHAPTER 18

Activities for Different Travelers

Solo Explorers: Customized excursions and opportunities for social interaction

Traveling solo through the Amalfi Coast, I discovered that this stunning locale is not just about breathtaking views but also about crafting an adventure that suits your personal taste and opens avenues for new friendships. Here, the solo explorer can dive into a myriad of customized excursions designed to not only explore the physical landscape but also to connect with others.

From Positano to Ravello, each town along the coast offers unique experiences tailored for individual discovery and group interaction. For instance, joining a group hike along the Path of the Gods not only challenges you physically but also places you amidst fellow wanderers, providing that perfect blend of solitude and companionship. The trails are well-marked, and local guides offer insights into the natural history and folklore, making every step educational as well as exhilarating. In Amalfi, the cooking classes at a local agriturismo are a favorite among solo travelers. Learning to prepare traditional dishes such as 'limoncello' using locally sourced lemons becomes not just a lesson in cooking but a social event, ending with a communal meal where stories and tips are exchanged over home-cooked delicacies. For those who yearn for sea adventures, sailing classes or group kayaking tours provide an exceptional way to meet people while learning a new skill. These activities are typically organized by local sports clubs which focus on safety and provide all necessary equipment, making them accessible even to the novice adventurer. Nightly, the small bars and cafes of Sorrento become hubs of interaction, where live music and dance evenings allow solo travelers to mingle with locals and other tourists in a relaxed, friendly atmosphere. Here, language is no barrier, as the universal appeal of music and dance draws everyone in.

The beauty of traveling solo on the Amalfi Coast lies in the seamless blend of independence and community. Each activity designed for solo travelers respects your space but also gently nudges you towards engaging with the world around you. Whether it's through a shared boat ride to Capri, a joint excursion to ancient ruins, or a casual gelato tasting session by the pier, the opportunities to forge new connections are as abundant as they are fulfilling. Navigating the coast is straightforward, with well-connected bus services and ferries linking the main towns. For those who prefer the scenic route, renting a scooter to wind through the coastal roads offers an exhilarating way to move from one picturesque village to another, stopping wherever and whenever a sight catches your eye.

Couples: Idyllic beach walks and exclusive dining experiences

Strolling hand in hand along the sun-dappled beaches of the Amalfi Coast, my partner and I found that every turn along the coastline offered a new slice of paradise, tailor-made for couples seeking both romance and adventure. The Amalfi Coast, with its juxtaposition of mountain and sea, quaint villages, and luxurious hideaways, provides an idyllic backdrop for couples to create memorable experiences together.

One of our first discoveries was the serene beaches of Positano, where the soft murmur of the waves and the spectacular view of the cliffside villas set the stage for perfect sunset walks. The beach at Fornillo, quieter than Positano's main beach, became a favorite spot for us to unwind and relish the peaceful ambiance, with just the sound of the sea as our company. Dining in Amalfi Coast, however, is an experience unto itself, transcending mere meals to become a celebration of love and life. We dined at La Sponda in Positano, illuminated by hundreds of candles, where the ambiance was as breathtaking as the meticulously crafted dishes. The restaurant, nestled in the luxurious Le Sirenuse Hotel, offers a menu that highlights local seafood and fresh ingredients from the region, all paired with a view that makes every dinner here linger in your memory long after the last bite.

For a truly exclusive dining experience, we ventured to Ravello, to the Belmond Hotel Caruso. Perched on a cliff overlooking the sparkling Mediterranean, this historic hotel offers a dining terrace where couples can enjoy a private candlelit dinner under the stars, surrounded by the scent of citrus from the nearby groves and the gentle whisper of the evening breeze. Every meal, every walk, and every moment on the Amalfi Coast seemed infused with an inherent romance and luxury, crafted over centuries to celebrate the union of nature and artistry. Whether it was a leisurely day spent exploring the hidden coves accessible only by private boats or an evening enjoying a live opera under the stars in the ancient gardens of Ravello, the experiences here are designed to deepen bonds and create joyful memories.

Accessibility along the coast is facilitated by the SITA buses and ferries linking the main towns, making it easy to explore this enchanting coastline. Many couples choose to rent scooters, adding a touch of adventure to their day as they navigate the scenic coastal road at their own pace, stopping at viewpoints that seem designed for stolen kisses and promises of forever.

Families: Attractions suitable for children and family-friendly park visits

Discovering the Amalfi Coast with my family was an enchanting experience, filled with child-friendly attractions and parks that made every day a new adventure. The region, known for its dramatic coastal views and picturesque towns, also caters wonderfully to families traveling with children, offering a mix of natural beauty, history, and engaging activities that can keep all ages entertained.

One of our first family excursions was to the ancient maritime republic of Amalfi. The town itself is compact and very walkable, which is perfect for families. We visited the Amalfi Cathedral, located right in the heart of the town square. The cathedral has a fascinating mix of architectural styles that span centuries, and the front steps provided a perfect spot for our family photo. Even our youngest was mesmerized by the colorful majolica tiles of the cathedral's roof.

Not far from Amalfi, we explored the Valle delle Ferriere, a nature reserve that offers a gentle yet adventurous hike suitable for older children. The trail winds through lush greenery, alongside streams and waterfalls, leading to ruins of old paper mills—one of Amalfi's historic industries. The cooler temperatures in the valley provided a pleasant break from the Mediterranean sun, and the kids loved watching the rare, indigenous plants and butterflies that thrive in this microclimate.

We also spent a delightful day at the Villa Rufolo in Ravello, which hosts family-friendly events, including outdoor concerts that are part of the Ravello Festival. The villa's gardens are a spectacle of their own, with vibrant flower beds and sweeping views of the coastline below. It's a splendid place for children to run and play amidst the open spaces, while adults can appreciate the historic architecture and the breathtaking panorama. For a beach day, we headed to Minori, a less crowded alternative to the more famous Positano and Amalfi beaches. Minori offers a lovely sandy beach with gentle waters, ideal for toddlers and young swimmers. The promenade behind the beach is lined with gelaterias and casual pizzerias, perfect for quick, kid-friendly meals. We enjoyed relaxed lunches here, with the kids happily digging into their pizzas and gelatos.

Getting around the Amalfi Coast with children was easier than expected, thanks to the local buses and ferries connecting the main towns. We occasionally rented a scooter with a sidecar for short, fun rides along the scenic coastal road. The kids absolutely loved the feeling of the wind in their hair as we scooted past the lemon groves and terraced vineyards. The Amalfi Coast is not just a romantic escape; it's a haven for families seeking a mix of relaxation and exploration.

Senior Travelers: Accessible cultural excursions and relaxing activities

Exploring the Amalfi Coast as a senior traveler brought a delightful ease to experiencing Italy's legendary beauty, all thanks to the accessible cultural excursions and relaxing activities tailored to those of us who enjoy a gentler pace. Here, the richness of life is savored in slow, scenic strolls and extended lunches under the Mediterranean sun, which I found wonderfully accommodating.

One of the most serene experiences was visiting the Villa Cimbrone in Ravello. Famous for its stunning gardens and panoramic views of the coastline, Villa Cimbrone offers well-maintained paths that are easy to navigate for those with mobility concerns. The highlight for me was the Terrace of Infinity, lined with busts that seem to gaze eternally over the sea. Access to the villa from Ravello's main square is facilitated by well-paved paths, making it a stress-free outing for seniors.

For accommodations, I stayed at the Hotel Marina Riviera in Amalfi, located at Via P. Comite, 19. Their contact number is +39 089 871104, and more details can be found at (mailto:info@marinariviera.it). This hotel stands out due to its accessibility features, including rooms equipped with safety bars in the bathrooms and minimal need for stair navigation, as elevators are available. Prices range from $250 to $400 per night, which reflects the premium amenities and accessibility. Situated just off the main street that runs along the coast, the hotel is conveniently located with direct access to Amalfi's charming town center and the seafront.

Dining out was also a highlight, and Ristorante Marina Grande, on Viale della Regione, 4, quickly became my favorite. Reach them at +39 089 871129 or visit (mailto:info@marinagrande.it). They offer an accessible dining room and an open terrace that overlooks the beach, making it an ideal spot for a leisurely dinner. The restaurant is renowned for its fresh seafood dishes and traditional Italian cuisine. With prices ranging from $30 to $60, it offers a delightful dining experience that caters to comfort and ease, with staff who are always ready to assist.

Traveling between the towns along the Amalfi Coast is made easier with the local SITA bus service, which provides accessible transportation with dedicated space for wheelchairs. Ferries also offer an enjoyable and scenic route between towns like Amalfi, Positano, and Sorrento, with staff prepared to assist in boarding and disembarking.

The Amalfi Coast is not just a destination; it's a gateway to a slower-paced, deeply cultural experience that cherishes accessibility. Whether it's the ease of getting around or the leisurely pace at which life unfolds here, the region welcomes senior travelers with open arms, ensuring that the beauty of the coast is accessible to all who visit.

Group Outings: Custom group adventures with special discounts

Embarking on a group adventure along the stunning Amalfi Coast, my friends and I discovered a trove of activities perfectly suited for fostering camaraderie and creating lifelong memories. The coast, with its serpentine shoreline and picturesque towns, offers a unique blend of natural beauty and Italian culture, enhanced by tailored group experiences and attractive discounts designed to make every outing special.

One of the highlights of our group journey was a custom boat tour operated by Amalfi Sails, located at Via Mauro Comite, 84011 Amalfi. You can reach them at +39 089 873344 or visit their website at (mailto:info@amalfisails.it). Their fleet includes a range of vessels from sleek sailboats to spacious yachts, all equipped for groups of various sizes. The cost of a private charter varies depending on the type of boat and duration of the trip, generally ranging from $500 for a half-day tour to S2,000 for a luxury yacht experience. The tour included stops at secluded beaches accessible only by water and a guided snorkeling excursion around the emerald waters near the Li Galli islands, known for their vibrant marine life.

For accommodations, we stayed at the Hotel Panorama, at Via Santa Tecla, 8, in Maiori. Contact them at +39 089 877122 or check their offerings at (mailto:info@hotelpanorama.it). This hotel is adept at handling large groups, offering rooms with balcony views and a generous breakfast buffet. Room rates for groups start around $100 per night per person, with discounts for bookings of ten or more. Its location makes it a perfect base for exploring nearby attractions, with easy bus and ferry connections. Dining as a group was a delight at La Taverna di Masaniello, situated at Via Pietro Capuano, 9, Amalfi. Their phone number is +39 089 871840, and more information can be found at (mailto:latavernadimasaniello@amalfi.it). The restaurant offers a special group menu featuring local specialties like spaghetti alle vongole and risotto alla pescatora, which range from $20 to $40 per person, including private dining areas for larger parties to enjoy a meal in comfort.

Custom group tours on land, such as guided hikes through the Valley of the Mills or cultural tours exploring historic sites like the Cathedral of Amalfi, cater to those interested in the rich history and stunning landscapes of the region. These tours are not only educational but also designed to accommodate the pace and interests of each group, with prices varying based on the length and scope of the tour, typically around $30 to $50 per person.

Group outings in the Amalfi Coast cater to all tastes and interests, combining the charm of Italy with the thrill of discovery in a group setting.

Guided Tours vs. Self-Guided Explorations

Navigating the splendid Amalfi Coast, I found myself torn between the structured support of guided tours and the thrilling autonomy of self-guided explorations. Each offers a unique way to experience this breathtaking region, and choosing the right path can deeply influence your travel experience.

Guided tours on the Amalfi Coast provide an enriching experience, especially for those visiting for the first time. These tours are led by knowledgeable local guides who offer invaluable insights into the history, culture, and hidden gems of the area. For example, Amalfi Coast Tours, located at Via Lorenzo d'Amalfi, 84011 Amalfi (contact: +39 089 831420; email: info@amalficoasttours.com), offers a variety of packages ranging from historical tours of ancient ruins to gastronomic tours featuring local cuisines. Prices typically range from $50 to $150 per person, depending on the tour's length and complexity. This company prides itself on small group sizes that allow for a personal and intimate experience, exploring spots like the Emerald Grotto and the hilltop terraces of Ravello.

On the other side, self-guided explorations offer freedom and flexibility, appealing particularly to the adventurous traveler. This option allows you to set your own pace and spend as much time as you desire at each location. Whether it's lingering in the fragrant lemon groves of Sorrento or meandering through the vibrant streets of Positano, you control the day. Resources for self-guided tours are plentiful, with downloadable maps and apps like "Amalfi Coast Path" providing detailed routes and cultural information. Costs for self-guided tours are often lower, mainly covering transportation and entry fees to certain sites, making it an economical choice.

Choosing between guided and self-guided tours often depends on your travel style. If you crave detailed stories about the places you visit and enjoy the convenience of pre-arranged transportation and entry, guided tours are unbeatable. However, if you prefer to immerse yourself in the local atmosphere at your own pace, without the constraints of a scheduled itinerary, then a self-guided tour might be your best choice.

One of the standout guided tour operators is Discover Amalfi Coast, located at Corso Reginna, 10, 84010 Maiori. You can reach them at +39 089 987 9999 or visit their website at (mailto:info@discoveramalficoast.com). They offer specialized tours like "Amalfi Lemon Tour," where you learn about the cultivation of lemons and even participate in making limoncello, priced around $70 per person, which includes tastings and a guided walk through lemon groves.

CHAPTER 19

Itineraries

Organizing Day Trips to Nearby Attractions

Discovering the Amalfi Coast through day trips is like unfolding the pages of a vividly illustrated storybook, each turn revealing panoramas and tales steeped in history. Let me guide you on how to organize memorable day excursions to nearby attractions, ensuring you capture the essence of this enchanting region.

Firstly, consider the logistical aspects. The coastal road, while breathtaking, is famously narrow and winding. Renting a scooter or a small car can give you the flexibility to explore at your pace. Alternatively, local buses are a reliable and scenic option, though they can get crowded during peak season. SITA buses connect most towns along the coast and are an economical choice. For those who prefer not to navigate the roads, guided tours available through local agencies offer a hassle-free way to see the sights, with added insights from knowledgeable locals. A must-visit is the town of Positano, a cascade of sun-bleached pink, peach, and terracotta colors. Starting your day early here allows you to wander through its steep streets and staircases without the midday crowds. Enjoy a leisurely breakfast at one of the seafront cafés before heading to the beach for a dip in the clear blue waters.

Next, head to the historic town of Amalfi. The majestic Amalfi Cathedral, situated at the top of a grand staircase, offers insights into the town's glorious past as a maritime powerhouse. The nearby Paper Museum, set in an old paper mill, provides a unique look at the traditional craft that once thrived here. If time permits, take a quick bus or a boat trip to Ravello, perched high above the coast. Known for its ravishing gardens at Villa

Rufolo and breathtaking views that have inspired artists and composers, Ravello is the perfect spot to reflect and unwind. Throughout your day trips, indulge in local cuisine. Savor a lunch featuring fresh seafood and try the famous limoncello, a sweet, potent liqueur made from the zest of Amalfi Coast lemons, which are said to be the largest and most flavorful due to the unique coastal climate.

Organizing these trips requires a bit of planning regarding transport and timing, but the rewards are immense. Each location offers a different slice of Amalfi life, from bustling beaches to quiet, flower-draped terraces. Always check the local transport schedules, as they can vary seasonally, and book your tickets or tours in advance during high season to avoid disappointment.

Brief Visits: Structured 3-Day Plans in Top Towns

Exploring the Amalfi Coast in just three days requires a bit of strategy to maximize the experience, and trust me, it's absolutely possible to soak in the essence of this stunning region in a short time. Let me walk you through a structured 3-day plan that highlights the best of Amalfi, Positano, and Ravello, blending iconic sights with some local secrets to make your visit truly memorable.

Day 1: Amalfi

Start your journey in Amalfi, the heart of the coast. Arrive early to enjoy a cappuccino at one of the cafés in Piazza del Duomo before the crowds arrive. The magnificent Amalfi Cathedral, with its striking façade and intricate bronze doors, is a must-visit. Take your time to explore the Cloister of Paradise, known for its Moorish influence and serene atmosphere. For lunch, grab a seat at a seaside restaurant to try some fresh seafood pasta—a local delicacy. In the afternoon, consider a boat tour to appreciate the coastline from the water, providing a different perspective and great photo opportunities of the cliffside villages.

Day 2: Positano

On your second day, head to Positano, the jewel of the coast known for its steep, narrow streets and vibrant colored houses stacked upon each other. Start with a stroll along Spiaggia Grande, the main beach, before wandering up the hill to explore the artisan shops. Positano is famous for its handmade leather sandals and colorful ceramics. For a truly unique experience, book a short cooking class with a local chef to learn how to prepare a traditional Neapolitan dish. As the sun sets, dine at a restaurant perched on the cliffs, where the views of the Mediterranean are as breathtaking as the food.

Day 3: Ravello

Conclude your trip with a day in Ravello, a quiet retreat perched high above the sea, offering panoramic views and a more relaxed pace. Visit the renowned Villa Rufolo, whose gardens inspired Wagner's Parsifal. Take your time to wander through the villa's gardens, which are often filled with music during the summer months thanks to the Ravello Festival. For lunch, try a trattoria in the town square, where you can savor local wines and simple, delicious cuisine. In the afternoon, take a leisurely walk along the "Path of the Gods," a hiking trail that offers some of the most spectacular vistas of the Amalfi Coast. This three-day itinerary allows for a full experience of the Amalfi Coast's diverse offerings—from historic sites and stunning views to gourmet meals and unique local crafts. Each day ends with an unforgettable sunset, whether viewed from a beach, a boat, or a mountain top, ensuring that your brief visit is as enriching as it is enchanting.

Extensive Weeklong Journeys: A Detailed 7-Day Guide

Embarking on a weeklong journey across the Amalfi Coast offers a chance to fully immerse oneself in the stunning landscapes, rich history, and vibrant culture of this iconic Italian riviera. Here's a detailed 7-day guide, crafted from my personal experiences, that ensures you soak in every bit of its enchantment, from serene sunrises over the Mediterranean to the bustling piazzas and quiet corners filled with the scent of lemon groves.

Day 1: Arrival and Amalfi Exploration

Start your adventure in Amalfi, the historic heart of the coast. Settle into your accommodation and then take a leisurely stroll through the town. Visit the majestic Amalfi Cathedral, with its striking mix of architectural styles, and wander through the ancient Cloister of Paradise. Dinner could be at a local trattoria, savoring dishes like scialatielli ai frutti di mare (seafood pasta).

Day 2: Ravello's Heights

On your second day, head up to Ravello, a hilltop retreat known for its breathtaking views and cultural richness. Visit the famed Villa Rufolo and Villa Cimbrone to wander through historic gardens and take in panoramic views that stretch across the coastline. In the evening, enjoy a concert if the Ravello Festival is in session—this is a must-do for classical music lovers.

Day 3: Positano's Charms

Day three brings you to Positano, the picture-perfect village known for its steeply stacked houses painted in a palette of peach, pink, and terracotta. Spend your day exploring the boutique shops, perhaps picking up handmade sandals or bespoke perfumes. Relax on the beach or rent a kayak to see the coast from the water. Dinner here means enjoying freshly caught fish while watching the sunset.

Day 4: Sorrento's Lively Culture

Travel to Sorrento for a change of pace. This larger town offers a vibrant mix of shopping, historical sites, and stunning sea views. Visit the Museo Correale for some art and history, and don't miss trying Sorrento's famous limoncello. Spend your evening at Piazza Tasso for some lively local interaction and a taste of Sorrento's nightlife.

Day 5: Capri by Boat

Take a ferry to the island of Capri for the day. Explore the iconic Blue Grotto, hike the Phoenician Steps up to Anacapri, or simply luxuriate in the glamorous atmosphere of the island. Enjoy a seaside lunch at one of Capri's renowned restaurants before heading back to the mainland.

Day 6: Nature's Call in the Valle delle Ferriere

Dedicate a day to nature by hiking the Valle delle Ferriere. This lesser-known trail leads you through lemon groves, dense forests, and past cascading waterfalls, offering glimpses of rare plants and perhaps some local wildlife. It's a refreshing contrast to the coastal views and gives a deeper appreciation of the region's diverse landscapes.

Day 7: Leisure and Departure

Your final day should be reserved for relaxation and last-minute explorations. Spend the morning revisiting a favorite spot or shopping for gifts. Enjoy a long lunch overlooking the sea, reflecting on your week's adventures. As the afternoon fades, prepare for your departure, filled with memories of a journey well spent. This itinerary blends iconic sights with unique experiences, ensuring a comprehensive exploration of the Amalfi Coast's offerings. Each day promises new sights and sensations, from the quiet awe of historic villas to the cheerful clamor of seaside villages, making every moment of your week here an unforgettable episode of your travel story.

2-Week Comprehensive Tour of the Amalfi Coast

Embarking on a two-week tour of the Amalfi Coast is the dream of many travelers, and having spent a glorious fortnight exploring its every nook, I can share a guide that delves deep into the region's beauty, culture, and adventures. This comprehensive itinerary ensures you experience the best of the Amalfi Coast, from serene mornings in quaint cafés to exhilarating boat rides and quiet evenings in lush gardens.

Week 1: Immersing in Coastal Marvels

Day 1-2: Amalfi

Start your journey in Amalfi itself. Spend your first day absorbing the vibrant atmosphere of this historic town. Visit the Amalfi Cathedral and its adjacent museum, wander through the charming streets, and sip limoncello on a sun-drenched terrace. The next day, explore the neighboring town of Atrani, a hidden gem just a short walk away, known for its authentic feel and less touristy vibe.

Day 3-4: Ravello
On the third day, head up to Ravello, perched high above the coast. The breathtaking views from Villa Rufolo and Villa Cimbrone are not to be missed. Spend a full day exploring these sites, perhaps attending a concert if timing coincides with the Ravello Festival. Enjoy a quiet evening at a local vineyard, tasting wines paired with views of the Mediterranean.

Day 5: Positano
Travel to Positano, famous for its stunning vertical landscape. Dedicate a day to leisurely exploring its steep streets, boutiques, and the beautiful church of Santa Maria Assunta. Relax on the beach or take a boat tour to nearby coves.

Day 6-7: Capri

Take a ferry to the island of Capri. Spend two days here, visiting the Blue Grotto, the Gardens of Augustus, and the Villa Jovis. Enjoy a sunset dinner at one of Capri's elegant restaurants, overlooking the Faraglioni rocks.

Week 2: Exploring Beyond the Usual

Day 8: Sorrento

Journey back to the mainland to Sorrento. Explore its historic center, the Museo Correale, and the marinas. Sorrento is also a great base for exploring local artisanal shops, where you can find inlaid woodwork and custom-made sandals.

Day 9-10: Pompeii and Mount Vesuvius

Dedicate a day to visiting the archaeological sites of Pompeii and Herculaneum, offering a poignant glimpse into ancient Roman life. The following day, hike Mount Vesuvius for a change of pace and panoramic views of the Bay of Naples.

Day 11: Paestum

Travel further afield to Paestum to admire some of the best-preserved Greek temples in Europe. Spend your time exploring the ruins, the museum, and the surrounding countryside.

Day 12-13: Lesser-Known Towns

Spend these two days in the lesser-known towns of the coast like Minori and Maiori, or venture into the hills to explore the villages of Scala and Tramonti. These places offer a more authentic slice of local life away from the main tourist hubs.

Day 14: Leisure and Departure

Use your last day to relax. Return to your favorite spot from the trip or discover a new one, like the quiet town of Sant'Agata sui Due Golfi, known for its spectacular views and excellent dining. Reflect on the journey, perhaps at a café overlooking the sea, journaling or planning your next visit.

This two-week itinerary on the Amalfi Coast blends iconic attractions with hidden gems, offering both relaxation and adventure. The coast's enduring charm lies not just in its famed scenery but also in its ability to offer a deeply personal connection to every traveler. Whether you're soaking in the sun on a secluded beach or tasting the rich flavors of Campanian cuisine, you'll find that the Amalfi Coast isn't just a place to visit—it's an experience to be cherished.

Free and Paid Tourist Attractions with Opening Hours

Exploring the Amalfi Coast is an adventure where every turn offers a picturesque vista, a hidden gem, or a historical marvel, with plenty of free and paid attractions to tailor your visit to your budget. From my days wandering these lush landscapes, I've gathered insights into how best to enjoy what the Amalfi Coast has to offer without missing out, regardless of how thick your wallet is.

One of the greatest pleasures here is simply soaking up the atmosphere. The town centers of Amalfi and Positano, with their vibrant street scenes and stunning beaches, are open to all. You can wander through the historic streets, relax on the public beaches, or hike the myriad of trails that offer breathtaking views across the coastline. The "Path of the Gods," a trail that links Agerola to Nocelle, is free and provides panoramic views that are among the most stunning in the world. It's typically open from dawn until dusk, depending on the season.

When it comes to paid attractions, the Amalfi Coast offers a range of historical sites and meticulously curated gardens that are well worth the entrance fee. For instance, the ancient Roman Villa in Minori, known as Villa Romana, charges around $5 for entry. It's open from 9 AM to 7:30 PM during the summer months, allowing visitors to explore extensive frescoes and ancient artifacts.

Ravello's renowned villas, Villa Rufolo and Villa Cimbrone, charge an entrance fee of $7 and $10 respectively. Villa Rufolo, famous for its stunning gardens that overlook the sea, is open from 8:30 AM to 8 PM in the peak season. Villa Cimbrone, on the other hand, is known for its iconic Terrace of Infinity and extensive English-style gardens, and its hours mirror those of Villa Rufolo.

In Amalfi, the Cathedral of Saint Andrew has a small fee of around $3 for access to the Cloister of Paradise, an architectural and artistic feast with exquisite Moorish influences. It's open from 9 AM to 5 PM, though times can vary slightly with the liturgical calendar.

For those interested in more curated experiences, boat tours to explore nearby caves and secluded beaches typically start at around $50 per person, offering a different perspective of the coast from the water. These tours usually run from 10 AM until sunset and provide all the equipment needed for snorkeling and sometimes even include a light meal. Whether you choose the free pathways cradled by wildflowers or the paid tranquility of ancient villas, each experience in Amalfi is imbued with its own unique flavor of culture, history, and stunning natural beauty. Always check the latest opening hours and book tickets in advance where possible, as this can save you time during the busy tourist season.

Departure Checklist and Customs Regulations

As my journey in the Amalfi Coast drew to a close, ensuring a smooth departure required more than just packing souvenirs and saying goodbye to the breathtaking views. Navigating through the customs regulations and ticking off my departure checklist were essential steps to make sure everything was set for an effortless return. Making sure my passport was valid for at least three months beyond my departure date was crucial, as this is a standard requirement for non-EU travelers. I also kept a copy of my accommodation details handy, which customs officers might request as proof of my stay.

Checking the weight and dimensions of my luggage was important to avoid hefty airline charges for excess baggage. I also made sure not to pack any prohibited items like certain cheeses or meats that might be restricted in my home country. For valuable items like electronics or jewelry that I declared upon entering Italy, I kept proof of this declaration to present during my departure to avoid any customs issues.

Understanding the EU's customs regulations helped streamline my experience. I was aware of the duty-free limits which generally allow 1 liter of spirits, 200 cigarettes, or 4 liters of wine. I also ensured any significant cultural artifacts purchased, like art or antiques, came from reputable dealers who provided the necessary export permits to prevent issues with Italy's laws against illegal trade of cultural heritage.

During my last day, I revisited charming boutiques for some last-minute gifts. I purchased a hand-painted ceramic vase in Positano, ensuring the shop provided me with a receipt and a statement for export. Arriving at Naples International Airport well ahead of time allowed a leisurely walk through the departure hall after checking my baggage and passing security. The customs officers were meticulous but fair, and having all documents prepared, including receipts for pricier items, facilitated a smooth process.

Reflecting on my departure from this magnificent coast, being well-prepared with knowledge of local and international regulations ensured my final memories were as peaceful as the beautiful days spent exploring. This preparation was key to a stress-free exit, avoiding any last-minute rushes or issues with customs, preserving the serene experience of my Amalfi Coast escape.

CHAPTER 20

Practical Information and Tips

Emergency Services: Medical Facilities and Contact Numbers

Visiting the Amalfi Coast, with its steep cliffs and breathtaking views, brings a certain tranquility that's often found in travel brochures and daydreams. Yet, amidst this serene backdrop, it's crucial to remember that emergencies can happen, and being prepared is key to ensuring they don't disrupt your beautiful escape.

From my own travels, I've learned that knowing the locations of medical facilities and having essential contact numbers can make all the difference. In the Amalfi Coast, you'll find several medical facilities that cater to everything from minor ailments to more urgent medical needs. For example, the Costa d'Amalfi Hospital in

Castiglione di Ravello offers comprehensive services and is equipped to handle a variety of medical situations. Their contact number, easily saved on your phone, is +39 089 683111.

Additionally, there are numerous pharmacies scattered throughout the towns, like Farmacia Centrale in Amalfi, located right in the heart of the town at Via Lorenzo d'Amalfi 29. They can be reached at +39 089 871324. Pharmacies in Italy are well-stocked and pharmacists often speak enough English to assist with common health issues.

For non-urgent medical advice, many hotels also offer doctor-on-call services, which can be reassuring if you're dealing with something less severe but still needing professional attention. Always check with your accommodation for the quickest way to access these services.

Moreover, it's wise to have the number for emergency services dialed into your phone. In Italy, the general emergency number is 112, which can connect you to medical, fire, and police assistance.

Navigating these practical aspects may not be the highlight of your trip, but having this information is like having a good map: it might not be needed at every turn, but it's invaluable when you really need to find your way. By ensuring you're prepared, you can rest easy and enjoy the breathtaking vistas and charming towns of the Amalfi Coast with peace of mind.

Consulates and Tourist Assistance in Italy

Traveling to the Amalfi Coast, with its mesmerizing vistas and historical richness, is a dream for many. As enchanting as the place is, navigating foreign lands always feels more reassuring when you know where to find consular support and tourist assistance, especially when you're miles away from home. From my experiences, having this information at your fingertips can significantly enhance your sense of security.

In Italy, each major city houses various consulates that can offer support to their nationals in case of emergencies like passport loss, legal troubles, or medical emergencies. For instance, the United States Consulate in Naples, located at Piazza della Repubblica, can be contacted at +39 081 583 8111. This proximity to the Amalfi Coast makes it accessible for American travelers seeking consular assistance.

For British tourists, the British Consulate in Naples offers similar services, aiding in emergencies and providing useful travel advice tailored to UK nationals. They are situated at Via dei Mille, 40, reachable via phone at +39 081 423 8911. These consulates typically operate during regular business hours, but they provide emergency contact numbers for after-hours situations.

Additionally, tourist assistance in the Amalfi Coast is remarkably comprehensive, designed to make visitors feel welcomed and supported. Tourist information offices are strategically located in almost every town along the coast. For example, Amalfi's tourist office can provide everything from local maps to event schedules and is conveniently located in the central Piazza del Duomo.

Moreover, Italy offers a unique service known as the "Carabinieri Tourist Police," who are specifically trained to assist tourists. They can help with reporting crimes, directing you to your consulate, or navigating local laws and regulations. Their presence is reassuring for any traveler facing unexpected challenges.

Remembering these details and contact points can transform your travel experience. Not only does it cushion you against potential travel hiccups, but it also lets you immerse fully in the vibrant life and spectacular scenery of the Amalfi Coast without undue stress. So, jot down these contacts, and set forth on your Italian adventure with confidence!

Special Occasion Planning: Weddings and Celebrations

Ah, the Amalfi Coast! If there ever was a perfect tapestry of turquoise waters, rugged cliffs, and lush lemon groves, this would be it. It's no wonder then that the Amalfi Coast ranks high on many dream lists for weddings and special celebrations. Planning a special occasion here, I found, is like setting a stage for an unforgettable romance or celebration steeped in Italian charm.

Wedding planners and event organizers in the Amalfi Coast are as plentiful as the picturesque views. They are masters in transforming the coastal beauty into a personalized event space. From intimate beachfront ceremonies to grand receptions in ancient villas overlooking the sea, the options are limitless. Villa Cimbrone in Ravello, for instance, offers a famous terrace, the Terrace of Infinity, which is ringed with statues and offers panoramic views of the Mediterranean. Its grounds provide a spectacular setting for wedding photos that seem to capture the very essence of romance.

Local cuisine also plays a central role in celebrations here. Imagine dining on fresh seafood, homemade pasta seasoned with locally grown herbs, and delectable pastries made from the famed Amalfi lemons — all of which are staples at wedding receptions and special dinners. Culinary teams often work with local ingredients to craft menus that are both a tribute to Italian culinary traditions and a personal reflection of the couple's tastes.

As for logistics, the Amalfi Coast, despite its steep cliffs and narrow roads, is surprisingly accessible for event guests. The nearest major airport is in Naples, from where private transfers can be arranged to whisk guests directly to their accommodations or to the event venue. Many choose to stay in cliffside hotels in Positano or

Amalfi, where balconies offer views that make every morning breathtaking.

But it's not just about the venues and the food; it's also about the atmosphere. There's something truly magical about saying your vows or celebrating a major milestone as the sun sets over the Mediterranean, casting a golden glow that seems to bless the occasion.

Planning an event here does require navigating local regulations and customs, so engaging a local planner is advisable. They handle everything from floral arrangements and music to legal paperwork, ensuring that your celebration not only runs smoothly but also infuses the local charm and spirit. In essence, celebrating a special occasion on the Amalfi Coast is about creating moments that, like the timeless beauty of the coast itself, will never fade in memory.

Photography Hotspots: Capturing the Perfect Shot

Exploring the Amalfi Coast, camera in hand, is like walking through a continuously unfolding tableau of vibrant scenes—each vying to be captured as a frame in my travel diary. From the sun-drenched lemon groves to the dramatic cliffs plunging into azure waters, photography enthusiasts will find no shortage of mesmerizing subjects here.

One of the most iconic shots, and a personal favorite, is from the town of Positano. The view from the main beach, looking back at the cliffside, offers a colorful cascade of buildings that perfectly captures the essence of this Italian jewel. To get here, a scenic drive along the SS163 brings you right into the heart of Positano. Early morning offers softer light and fewer crowds, making it ideal for that postcard-perfect shot.

Another not-to-miss spot is the Fiordo di Furore, a hidden sea cove nestled between cliffs. The bridge crossing the fjord provides a stunning composition with the turquoise sea below. It's easily accessible by SITA bus from Amalfi, and a morning visit captures the magical light without the midday sun's harshness.

For those captivated by heights, the Path of the Gods offers unparalleled vistas of the coast. Starting from Agerola, a bus from Amalfi will drop you at the trailhead. As you hike towards Positano, each turn presents a new panoramic view, with early spring or late autumn offering clear, crisp skies for distant shots of Capri and the vast sea.

Ravello, high above the coastal din, is a haven for capturing lush gardens and expansive seascapes. Villa Rufolo and Villa Cimbrone are both celebrated for their spectacular gardens that overlook the Mediterranean. The best time to visit is during the golden hour, when the light accentuates the vibrant flowers and the sea glows warmly. Ravello can be reached by bus from Amalfi, and wandering through these historic villas feels like stepping into a living painting.

Lastly, for those seeking a blend of history and scenery, the town of Amalfi itself offers narrow, bustling streets leading to the impressive Amalfi Cathedral. The steps of the cathedral are a fantastic spot for capturing the town's vibrant life. Arriving by bus or ferry, you're deposited right into the center of this bustling hub.

Each of these spots has its own unique charm, offering endless opportunities to capture the allure of the Amalfi Coast. Whether it's the sweeping panoramas from mountain trails or the intricate details of historic architecture, carrying my camera through these locales not only allowed me to document stunning visuals but also to truly connect with the spirit of this enchanting coast.

Sustainable Tourism Practices on the Amalfi Coast

On my journey along the Amalfi Coast, the fragrant lemon groves and terraced vineyards are not just a feast for the eyes—they're part of a deeply rooted culture that's leaning into sustainable tourism practices. The region is not only famed for its breathtaking views but also for its local communities' commitment to preserving this slice of paradise.

The Amalfi Coast is delicate; its beauty is unmistakable but its ecosystem is fragile. Over the years, local businesses, guided by the necessity to protect their heritage, have embraced sustainability as a core value. For instance, many hotels and resorts now prioritize green building standards and energy efficiency. It's common to find accommodations that use solar panels, rainwater harvesting systems, and organic products. In Positano, I stayed at a lovely boutique hotel that sources almost all its produce locally—right down to the soap made with olive oil from nearby groves.

Sustainable transport is another crucial aspect. The narrow, winding roads here are not built for heavy traffic, which makes public transportation a better option for the environment and often a quicker one for getting around. The local SITA buses connect most towns, and many areas are also well-serviced by ferries which offer a scenic route along the coast without the carbon footprint of car travel.

Diving into local culinary traditions here doesn't just tickle the palate; it supports local agriculture. Restaurants often showcase dishes made with ingredients like anchovies from Cetara and lemons from Amalfi—produce that hasn't traveled far to plate, thus cutting down on carbon emissions. During a dinner in a small trattoria in Ravello, each course was paired with a story of local sourcing, emphasizing the community's pride in its sustainable agriculture. Moreover, the Amalfi Coast's marine and land reserves play a significant role in conservation efforts. The Protected Marine Area of Punta Campanella, accessible via guided tours, is a model of marine biodiversity conservation. These tours not only offer a chance to explore the rich underwater life but also educate visitors on the importance of marine habitats and what can be done to protect them.

Visiting the Amalfi Coast isn't just about enjoying its natural and cultural offerings; it's also about participating in a movement towards sustainability. Every choice made here, from supporting local artisans to opting for eco-friendly tours, contributes to a larger effort of conservation that seeks to ensure this landscape can be enjoyed by generations to come. Through these experiences, it becomes clear that sustainable tourism is not just a practice but a celebration of local heritage and an investment in the future.

CONCLUSION

As my journey along the Amalfi Coast comes to a close, I'm left reflecting on the incredible blend of natural beauty, rich history, and vibrant culture that this stunning region has offered. From the sun-drenched lemon groves to the dramatic cliffside vistas, each moment here has felt like stepping into a beautifully painted postcard that no camera could fully capture.

This coast is not just a destination; it's an experience that engages all the senses. The salty air, the sound of the waves crashing against rocky shores, and the taste of fresh seafood pasta as the sun sets over the Mediterranean—these are memories that will linger long after my departure. The warmth of the local people, who share their traditions and stories with pride and joy, adds a depth to the visit that goes beyond the visual delights. In navigating the narrow, winding roads from Positano to Ravello, or boarding a ferry to the enchanting island of Capri, I've discovered that the Amalfi Coast offers a unique opportunity to slow down and savor each moment. Whether it's the quiet contemplation in a hilltop garden or the thrill of discovering hidden coves by kayak, the region encourages a pace of life that is both exhilarating and profoundly relaxing.

But this journey has also been an education. It's taught me the importance of preserving such a fragile environment through sustainable tourism practices. The local efforts to maintain the coastline, manage waste responsibly, and promote eco-friendly tourism are not just commendable but critical for ensuring that future visitors can enjoy the same enchanting experiences.

As I prepare to depart, checking off my travel checklist and ensuring I adhere to local customs regulations, I know that the Amalfi Coast has given me more than just beautiful photos and delicious meals. It has enriched me, challenged me to think about my impact as a traveler, and inspired me with its resilient, passionate locals who cherish and protect their cultural heritage.

So, to anyone reading this, who dreams of visiting the Amalfi Coast, know that what awaits you is more than a vacation. It's a chance to be part of a place where every view has a story, every meal is a celebration, and every step is an adventure. And when you do visit, tread lightly, respect the local ways of life, and embrace all that this magnificent coastline has to offer. You'll return home, not just refreshed, but transformed.

Made in the USA
Las Vegas, NV
26 March 2025

20135164R00167